A JUST SOCIETY?

A JUST SOCIETY?

Ethics and Values in Contemporary Ireland

Edited by
John Scally

The Liffey Press

Published by
The Liffey Press Ltd
Ashbrook House, 10 Main Street
Raheny, Dublin 5, Ireland
www.theliffeypress.com

A catalogue record of this book is
available from the British Library.

ISBN 1-904148-26-3

Printed in the Republic of Ireland by Colour Books Ltd.

CONTENTS

LA PILAR

For over twenty years, the world of Kathryn and Jamie Sinnott has been a world of pain, bewilderment, courage and perseverance. Kathryn, a personification of "Mother Courage", describes her life in two phases: BJ and AJ — "Before Jamie" and "After Jamie". Jamie was only three months old when he first began to exhibit symptoms of autism.

For twenty-five years Kathryn has campaigned to ensure that no more young people will ever have to "share the scrapheap with Jamie" and, like him, arrive at eighteen uneducated. She has struggled to persuade the health and education authorities to recognise autism and provide appropriate education and training for those with it. She has evoked the country's admiration because she has done so, in the words of the High Court, "in the face of official indifference and persistent procrastination". Despite the many setbacks she has had on the way, she remains defiant and determined to continue her battle for educational rights for the disabled, whatever their age.

Jamie's situation has long since ceased to be just about Jamie. With this in mind, Kathy is developing La Pilar, Integrated Early Learning Research and Training Centre, to help infants and children experiencing developmental delay. To do this, she is assembling comprehensive facilities and a range of professionals to meet their needs. Early response to the challenge of a primary disability maximises a child's ability and prevents the development of tragic and avoidable secondary disablement. The centre will cater for children from birth to school entrance.

If you would like further information on La Pilar, contact 021-4888503.

Royalties from this book will go to La Pilar.

ABOUT THE CONTRIBUTORS

Mary Banotti became one of the best-known faces in Irish political life when she contested the Presidential election in 1997. She is a grand-niece of Michael Collins. She was educated by the Dominican sisters and after school she took up a career in nursing. She is currently a Member of the European Parliament.

David Begg is General Secretary of the Irish Congress of Trade Unions. In addition to his long commitment to the trade union movement, he also served as Chief Executive of Concern.

Fr Harry Bohan founded the Rural Housing Organisation in 1972, in an attempt to stem mass emigration, and in the process seeking to preserve and develop local rural communities throughout the west of Ireland. He founded the Céifin Institute to reflect, debate and direct values-led change in Irish society. He also managed the Clare county hurling team, leading them to consecutive National League titles in 1977 and 1978.

Dr Leonard Condren is a medical graduate of UCD and has spent all of his professional working life in his native city of Dublin. He has practised as a GP since 1980 and has been a regular contributor to various Irish medical publications. Currently he is the medical editor of irishhealth.com, the award-winning health information website. Dr Condren job-shares his clinical work with his wife Mary, who is also a GP.

Deirdre de Burca is a Green Party Councillor in Bray. She ran as a candidate in the General Election in Wicklow in May 2002. A trained psychologist, she worked for the Rehab Group for twelve years. She has a keen interest in equality issues in the broadest sense.

Ubaldus de Vries studied law at the University of Leiden and wrote his PhD in Ireland, at Dublin City University. He now teaches law in the Faculty of Law at Utrecht University, The Netherlands.

Richard Douthwaite is an internationally acclaimed writer on environmental and economic matters. He lives in the West of Ireland.

Dermot Earley played senior football for Roscommon for twenty years and is universally recognised as one of the greatest players never to win an All-Ireland medal. He is a senior officer in the army and served for four years in New York as the Military Advisor to the Secretary-General of the United Nations.

John Feehan is a senior lecturer in the Department of Environmental Resource Management at University College Dublin, where much of his research and teaching centres on environmental heritage evaluation and management. He is well known for his television work on the natural and cultural heritage of the Irish landscape, for which he received a Jacobs Television Award. His *History of Farming in Ireland* is currently in press.

Bishop Christopher Jones is Bishop of Elphin. He played a significant role in the development of social services in Sligo in the 1970s and was actively involved in the pastoral care of the Travelling community. He is also a campaigner for the ongoing development of the west of Ireland.

Sr Stanislaus Kennedy has long been a prophetic voice against injustice in Ireland. She is the director of Focus Ireland.

Archdeacon Gordon Linney was born in Dublin in 1939. He was educated at High School in Dublin and worked with the Royal Bank before entering Church of Ireland Theological College to train for ordination. He was appointed Rector of Glenageary in 1980 and Archdeacon of Dublin in 1988. He has represented the Church of Ireland in various aspects of the Northern Ireland peace process. He is a regular broadcaster and contributor to the media.

John Lonergan is Governor of Mountjoy Prison and contributes frequently to the media on a wide variety of social topics.

Fr Seán McDonagh was ordained a priest in 1969 and spent the following years in parish and teaching ministry in the Philippines as a Columban missionary. From 1980 onwards, he worked among the T'boli people of South Cotabato and at this time his concern for the destruction of the environment grew. He is the author of numerous books and articles about the environment.

Finian McGrath was elected as a TD for Dublin North Central in May 2002. The former teacher was one of eight independent candidates who were contesting the general election as Independent Health Alliance. For years, he had been an ardent campaigner for the rights of the disabled in Ireland.

Peter McVerry SJ is a Jesuit priest. For years he has championed the cause of the marginalised in Irish society. He is particularly associated with the campaign to provide accommodation for homeless boys.

Gina Menzies is one of Ireland's leading commentators on religious and social affairs. She is a frequent contributor to RTE radio and television and the printed media. She has lectured extensively on ethical and theological issues.

Martin O'Donoghue, a former Economics Professor at TCD, was Minister for Education and Minister for Economic Planning and Development in Jack Lynch's cabinet from 1977 to 1979.

Feargal Quinn is executive chairman of Superquinn and an independent member of Seanad Éireann.

Annie Ryan is a former president of the National Association for Mentally Handicapped of Ireland and has been a tireless campaigner for the rights of people with disabilities. She is author of *Walls of Silence*, an account of attitudes to people with a mental disability and of the dealings of successive governments in this area.

Trevor Sargent is the leader of the Green Party. He is an active member of the Church of Ireland. He also has a keen interest in the Irish language.

John Scally lectures in the Department of Hebrew, Biblical and Theological Studies in Trinity College. He is the author of a number of books on ethics and on sport.

Frank Shouldice is a freelance journalist and playwright/director for theatre, film and television. He has written extensively on social issues, travel, arts and sports for national newspapers in Ireland and both scripted and presented radio for RTE's *World Report*. Last year he co-wrote, with Fr Harry Bohan, *Community and the Soul of Ireland: The Need for Values-Based Change*.

Kathryn Sinnott almost caused a seismic shock in Irish politics when after two recounts she came within six votes of taking a seat from Fianna Fáil in the 2002 General Election. A mother of nine children, she campaigns for people with disabilities.

Dedication
To Mary and Shane Minogue

INTRODUCTION

John Montague brilliantly remembered his childhood in the line "Like dolmens around my childhood the old people". It is a phrase which resonates deeply for me because my window into the world was — and to some extent remains — my grandfather. The dead are our closest companions. When I was a boy he told me that if I ever wanted to judge a man's character, the best way to do it was to examine the way he treated his horse. It was great advice at the time but sadly it is not very helpful today as the horse and cart are no more.

The rural Ireland where I was born no longer exists: a society where ethics generally consisted of a fairly routine obedience to powerful personalities and structures. With brutal suddenness, these powers have been severed. Ireland has gone through a massive socio-cultural change in the last few decades and that inevitably impacts on the way we think and talk about ethics. Our country has changed too fast too quickly to be easily understood.

Another thing about the enormity and speed of the cultural changes is that many of our touchstones of meaning and values like religion and community no longer seem to have the power they used to. To take one example, I was brought up in a culture with a strong sense of symbol through benediction and the May altars. In our culture of MTV, McDonalds and Pepsi is there any place for symbol any more? Or do we live in age of imaginative emptiness?

It is still too early to assess how Ireland has changed because of the Celtic Tiger but it is probably safe to quote Yeats: "all has changed, changed utterly". Has a "terrible beauty" been born?

These socio-cultural changes impacted profoundly, but subtly, on our value system. For example, one of the healthier legacies of the education system bequeathed by the religious orders in Ireland was the inclusion of the value of service alongside personal development, emotional satisfaction, monetary reward and occupational status, as the goals of education. With the decline of religious in teaching, a shift appears to have taken place. There remains an emphasis on personal achievement and personal quality but notions of communal purpose and social value have abated.

The words of Václav Havel seem remarkably applicable to the Ireland of 2003:

> Today, many things indicate that we are going through a transitional period when it seems that something is on the way out and something else is painfully being born. It is as if something were crumbling, decaying and exhausting itself, while something else, still indistinct, were arising from the rubble.

This transition brings a plethora of ethical dilemmas that call into question many of our traditionally cherished values.

As a teenager, the first politician to make an impression on me was Garret Fitzgerald. His idealism was particularly infectious when he spoke so passionately about the need to create "a just society". Twenty years on, does the idea of a just society still seem as distant a dream as it did in the bleak 1980s?

One difficulty is that a reflection on the changing Irish society is a luxury not every one can afford to entertain. As the great Samuel Johnson wrote, "A man doubtful of his dinner or trembling at a creditor is not much disposed to abstracted meditation." For those on the margins of our society who have found the Celtic tiger to be not even a Celtic pussycat, the discussion in this book might seem a little removed from their reality.

Despite the great economic success we have enjoyed, the gulf between rich and poor continues to widen. Spiralling house prices will ensure this inequality exacerbates. While thankfully there have been great advances in recent years in many areas of Irish life, not all the changes have been to our advantage. The "Ireland of the thousand welcomes" is dead and hastily buried in a pauper's grave. Indeed, our Travelling community might well have grounds to ask was it ever anything but a figment of our imagination. Given the apartheid, Irish-style, which they have been subjected to, they must find the phrase "fellow citizens" nothing more than a bad joke.

Human life is problematic, insofar as life proceeds by decisions, which we take at a particular time. To become human involves more than merely reacting to stimuli; we are molded by the fundamental values, principles and rules which take on life when we act in freedom, that is when we act in a particular way and give our personal allegiance to that choice. It is because we *can* shape our lives that questions arise about how we should do so. But who should direct us in making these choices? Do we look for guidance from our political elite?

Poverty is endemic in many areas of Irish society but perhaps the most serious poverty is the poverty of leadership. Who is really steering the future of Irish society? In whose interests? To what agenda? Ireland used to be the island of saints and scholars. Now it is the island of sleaze and corruption. Politics, banking, the church, business, the planning process, the medical profession and the Gardaí have all suffered from an erosion of public confidence in the wake of an astonishing proliferation of scandals. In the light of all the scandals and the profound changes in Irish society, it is important for us to reflect systematically on ethics in Ireland today.

In its broadest sense, ethics refers to what is good and bad, to questions of right and wrong. Ethics, in the western world, since the time of its inception with Socrates, has been a philosophical endeavour, designed to determine which guides for action are worthy of acceptance and for what reasons.

The approach which I will be working from understands ethics as the systematic study of the fundamental principles and key concepts that are or ought to be found in any given field of human activity and thought. Ethicists respond to the nature of human activity, which involves a choice. Such analysis involves a vast range of human activity. This is best illustrated by a practical example. In urban areas, in certain climatic conditions, the decision as to whether or not to light a coal fire is ethically significant because the fumes from the fire could lead to smog, thus affecting the living conditions and even health of people. This example highlights the fact that every human decision is ethically significant.

Most of our decisions are made without the luxury of having considerable time to tease out the ethical implications of all our actions. Thus some general framework of ethical reflection is essential to assist people to make speedy decisions in ordinary professional or domestic circumstances.

THE GLOBAL VILLAGE

It seems to me that the popular idea of our world as a global village is profoundly misleading because village has connotations of intimacy, community and solidarity. I think that the poet Micheal O'Siadhail is much closer to the mark when he writes of a "Fragile City" with all its connotations of delicate social networks and loneliness. Obviously, 11 September 2001 gives a new poignancy to that phrase.

Of course, an additional dimension to the "problem" is that we live in an increasingly pluralistic culture. As Jonathan Sacks perceptively observed, "Society has taken on the character of Salman Rushdie's definition of literature: voices talking about everything in every possible way."

Given the enormity and speed of the changes in Irish society, it is an opportune time to begin some process of a communal self-examination. This book is intended to make a modest contribution to the reflection that must take place at this time of turbulent transition and to hopefully raise the agenda for further debate. Are there any values that we can honestly say we share anymore? If so, what are they? If not, why not? Does Irish society today suffer from a sense of dis-ease?

To assist me in this process, I have recruited a number of distinguished contributors. Rather than going for "hurlers on the ditch", I have opted for people working "at the coalface" in particular areas. They bring the authority of their lived experience to this project. It is a tribute to the depth of their understanding that they do not always agree with one another.

To begin, Sr Stanislaus Kennedy, in a wide-ranging article, points to some of the issues that we must collectively confront.

Of course, ethical issues are not just questions for Irish society and cannot be definitively answered without reference to the European context. The Laken Declaration on the Future of the European Union in December 2001 posed the question of Europe's new role in a globalised world:

> Beyond its borders, in turn, the European Union is confronted with a fast-changing, globalised world. Following the fall of the Berlin Wall, it looked briefly as though we would for a long while be living in a stable world, free from conflict, founded upon human rights. Just a few years later, however, there is no such certainty. The eleventh of September has brought a rude awakening. The opposing forces have not gone away — religious fanaticism, ethnic nationalism, racism and terrorism are on the increase, and regional conflicts, poverty and underdevelopment still provide a constant seedbed for them . . .
>
> Now that the Cold War is over and we are living in a globalised, yet also highly fragmented world, Europe needs to shoulder its responsibilities in the governance of globalisation. The role it has to play is that of a power resolutely doing battle against all violence, all terror and all fanaticism, but which does not turn a blind eye to the world's heartrending injustices. In short, a power wanting to change the course of world affairs in such a way as to benefit not just the rich countries but also the poorest. A power seeking to set globalisation within a moral framework, in other words to anchor it in solidarity and sustainable development.

Mary Banotti MEP considers the issue of a just society in the context of the Boston-Berlin debate.

MONEY, MONEY, MONEY

Any consideration of the just society must by necessity reflect on the economy generally and the role of the business community specifically. Business today is conducted in an environment which is complex, competitive and demanding; many people question if it is possible to conduct business in an ethically responsible way. The award-winning film *Wall Street* popularised the slogan, "greed is good"; is there any justification for this opinion? Over recent years, a proliferation of scandals have arisen both in national and international contexts which provoked widespread concern. Such scandals did not occur in a vacuum but are symptoms of a deeper underlying malaise in contemporary society. An economic system which causes unsavoury practices to develop in the first place must be reformed. The challenge today is to formulate a new vision of the economic order which does justice to the interests not only of the business corporation, employees, entrepreneurs and customers but also those of the marginalised and society itself. A central part of this vision is to articulate a new approach to profit, which allows business people to obtain a just reward for the initiative and effort but which sees profit as a means to an end rather than as an end in itself. Profit, and the economic order in general, need to advance the good of the many and not just the wealthy few.

But when is the price of additional wealth creation too high? How are we to balance the risk of destruction or pollution, for example, with the creation of additional jobs? What criteria are to be used in deciding if the price of progress is too high? Who is to decide? How is wealth to be distributed? Such questions point to the need for a vigorous examination and critique of the economic system. It is only against this wider background that a detailed consideration of business ethics can take place.

A systematic approach to business ethics must reflect on the inter-relationships between the personal, the institutional and the societal dimensions of business. At one level, business ethics focuses on the development of the personal qualities needed to live and work with virtue and integrity. At another level, the challenge is to formulate a critical analysis of business corporations and financial institutions which does justice to their legitimate expectations and the good of humankind.

At a further level, the analysis of the personal and corporate dimensions of business ethics must be integrated into a wider discussion of "the market society" where business transactions are completed. Such analysis is greatly impoverished without a consideration of the strengths and weaknesses of the market system as a system of social co-ordination, extending to an analysis of the multinational companies and trading patterns on the people in the developing world.

David Begg considers the distribution of wealth in Ireland in the wider context of the global economic order and argues cogently that we need a market economy rather than a market society.

Former Minister for Economic Planning and Development and Professor of Economics Martin O'Donoghue views the capitalist system in a different light in his discussion of the ethical issues involved in the distribution of wealth. He contends that, despite the recent wave of business scandals, there is no inherent conflict between making profits and acting in the public interest. Senator Feargal Quinn brings his long years in business to his consideration of the issue of "Profit versus the Public Good".

Peter McVerry SJ uses a parable to illustrate how the Celtic tiger has impacted on different groups in Irish society in contrasting ways. He argues that the soul of ethics is a sense of solidarity and presents his vision of a just society. John Lonergan also draws on his long experience of dealing with the marginalised in his quest for a more just society.

CARING FOR THE EARTH

One area in which business has a particular role to play is in ensuring that the creation of wealth is not at the expense of the destruction of the environment.

No ethicist would dissent from Winston Churchill's assertion, stripped from its ideological baggage, that: "It is a socialist idea that making profit is a vice. I consider the real vice is making losses." The ethical problem arises when profit becomes an end in itself and when the gains of the greedy are at the expense of the pains of the needy or of the environment. There is evidence to suggest that the western world has recklessly squandered the resources of the world and exploited developing economies for their selfish gain. The social cost of this economic activity is to be seen in environmental destruction. Part of the task of ethics is to consider how we meet the needs of the present without compromising the ability of future generations to meet their needs. Supporters of this view find an unlikely champion in Margaret Thatcher, who pointed out in 1988: "No generation has a freehold on this earth. All we have is a life tenancy — with a full repairing lease." Against this background, Fr Sean McDonagh considers ecology and ethics, focusing on genetic engineering and climate change; John Feehan probes our understanding of science in his reflection on ethics and the environment; Richard Douthwaite challenges us to develop an economic system that would permit growth to stop in the interests of the environment; while Trevor Sargent offers a short personal reflection on the need for an ethic of interdependence.

HEAVEN AND EARTH

The late Brendan Behan, on seeing a copy of the *Catholic Standard* in a bookshop, remarked: "Ah, here is the news of the next world." This is a revealing observation, highlighting as it does the way in which many Christians think of the church's purpose, i.e. to prepare our souls here in this world for the next world. The manner of Jesus' birth suggests otherwise, as from the outset He publicly aligned Himself with the poor and the outcasts. The church which Jesus called for therefore was a radical presence which empowered all people to have a meaningful life.

Can we look to the Christian Church for guidance to help us construct a just society? It too has had its credibility severely diminished. Hence the need for a serious consideration of the moral authority of the Church today.

Archdeacon Gordon Linney in his wide-ranging article, "The Church and a Just Society", grounded in contemporary Irish society, opts for an approach that is very different from Behan's as he delineates the challenges facing the churches in Ireland "struggling with a process of change that is both disturbing and challenging". Bishop Christopher Jones takes on a similar task.

Fr Harry Bohan focuses on the need "to develop a coherent set of values that can give us a sense of unity and purpose, a vision for the future and the ability to decide what quality of life we want for ourselves".

The family is of central importance in the Irish constitution. But, given the complexities and ambiguities in Irish society today, what do we mean by family any more? Gina Menzies takes up the question of justice in family relationships in her article.

THE EQUALITY AGENDA

A number of questions present themselves about the place of disabled people in 2003. In Irish society, are all people equal, or are some, like the disabled, seen as less equal than others? How many disabled people are institutionalised? How many have a home of their own? How many have access to the special education that they may require? How many have a job? Kathy Sinnott is ideally placed to comment on our attitudes to the disabled. Annie Ryan gives her account of an ongoing struggle for a health system that is grounded on justice.

Such discussion inevitably raises major questions about politics and ethics. Thomas Moore famously said that he would "die the king's good servant but God's first". For the theologian Fichter, "service to the nation is the route to immortality". So what political response do we need today? Finian McGrath TD shares his thoughts on this subject, inspired in part by his own experiences.

As equality issues come to the fore, there is a need for a new approach which takes account of the need to build new relationships of mutuality and reciprocity between women and men. Many women echo the type of sentiments expressed by the former Irish president Mary Robinson in her inauguration speech in 1990:

> As a woman I want women who have felt themselves out-
> side of history to be written back into history, in the words
> of Eavan Boland, finding a voice where they found a vision.

Deirdre de Burca reminds us that there is still work to be done to
secure genuine equality in Ireland.

BAD MEDICINE?

The two great constants of human existence — birth and death —
were for centuries a matter for God and nature only. Now science
has intervened. Never before have the possibilities open to humankind been so great, and yet hand in hand with these exciting
developments in science and health care a certain fear has taken
root, a fear of what might be called the dehumanisation of medicine. A consequence of the increasing technology is that the traditional ethical question has been turned on its head. Historically,
ethicists have asked the question: how can people be brought to
do what they ought? Today, particularly as cloning seems now an
option, increasingly ethicists are asking: when should people be
restrained from doing all that they are capable of? How are we to
shield ourselves from the excesses of technical advances in medicine while preserving the benefits of modern health care? How
can we ensure that our knowledge and our needs remain in step?
How are we to keep science from encroaching on our rights and
dignity while nurturing basic values and ethical principles?

The inherent trust which is an essential element in the relationship between doctors and their patients has been threatened
by recent controversies — notably the revelation that Irish hospitals were harvesting the organs of dead children without the consent of their parents and the scandal which caused many people
to acquire Hepatitis C or HIV from contaminated blood. Who will
ever forget the distressing details of the Brigid McCole case?

In Ireland, there appears to be a shift from a social to an economic view of medicine. There is an increasing dichotomy between the super-specialist and primary health care producers.
Medicine has changed and continues to change rapidly. Society

has undergone profound changes. Yet the value system which underlines medical ethics essentially dates back over two thousand years. Is this a satisfactory situation? Dr Leonard Condren offers a personal view of medical ethics and points to the need to expand the horizons of the doctors of the future by emphasising the ethical dimension to conducting a medical consultation.

Difficult ethical issues in medicine are increasingly resolved in the courts. Further painful questions lie in store for us in this area, which will inevitably challenge our value system. As a taster of the problematic issues that await us around the corner, Ubaldus de Vries asks: can a legal right to euthanasia exist?

SOUND AND VISION

Any systematic consideration about ethics must consider the role of the media in Irish society. The Green Paper on broadcasting in the 1990s asked a very provocative question: "Is RTE too Dublin-orientated?" This is an important issue. As someone born and bred in the west of Ireland, I am acutely aware that many people feel condemned to the margins, to be no more than exiles at the far end of solitude in terms of having their views represented in the national media.

In the run up to the Maastricht referendum in 1992, the buzz phrase was the "democratic deficit", i.e., the belief that so called "ordinary people" were denied access to the political process. Is there a similar deficit in terms of access to the media? This whole area is an ethical equivalent of a Pandora's box. Whose truth? Which truths? Who decides which facts and stories deserve to be reported and using what criteria?

It is important to recognise that the media has the legitimate task of bringing information to the public. In fact, in the Irish context, it was largely the media who had the courage to rip aside all the curtains of hypocrisy and to expose the cruel reality behind the mirages of our traditional images of the political, business and religious establishment. Moreover, the media ought not be used as a blanket term. The paparazzi apparently inhabit a very different ethical world to such wonderful journalists as Maggie O'Kane and Fergal Keane.

In the print media, there is disquiet about a certain style of journalism. These are opinion pieces which seem to serve no other purpose than to sneer at particular public figures. On the day of Princess Diana's death, a diarist in an English newspaper joked that if she had an IQ five points lower she would have to be watered every day. One commentator has described this trend as the "culture of contempt". Such articles may not be unethical but they are at the very least questionable.

What has happened is not so much that the media have been unconcerned about whether or not they were making responsible use of their knowledge and skill. The real problem is that mutually inconsistent forms of ethical evaluation have come into play, but this inconsistency and the inadequacy of some of the approaches have not being recognised. There are important ethical questions for society at large about the role of the media. The debate is embryonic and must be carefully nuanced. Frank Shouldice offers his thoughts on this important issue.

Finally, sport plays a huge role in Irish life today but what ethical system, if any, does it reflect? Is it about winning at all costs? Legendary Roscommon footballer Dermot Earley and I reflect on ethics and sport.

I am very grateful to all the contributors for supporting this project, and to David Givens and Brian Langan at The Liffey Press for their practical assistance.

It often seems to me that the most important things in Irish society are those that are least talked about. Hopefully, this book can in a small way counter-act this tendency. Accordingly, I invite readers to join us, in the words of St Thomas Aquinas, *"in dulcedine societatis quaerere veritatem"* — "to seek the truth in the sweet harmony of fellowship".

1

A NEW CONSCIENCE FOR OUR TIME

Stanislaus Kennedy RSC

The society we have in Ireland today is a legacy of the sacrifices made by previous generations, who experienced poverty and want, in order to create a better future for their children — but is it the kind of liberated society they dreamed of? Certainly we have massively increased wealth and opportunities, yet for many Irish people it has been anything but a source of liberation. Indeed it has failed to equip many of our people with the basic building blocks for a fulfilled and successful adult life.

I am thinking here of the thousands of Irish people who have gone through primary and second-level schools but who are unable to write or who can do so only very poorly. I am thinking of the 17 per cent of our children who still live in consistent poverty and the 8 per cent of our adult population who live in chronic poverty. I am thinking of the neglect of thousands who are homeless, on housing waiting lists and on hospital waiting lists. I am thinking of the neglect of groups such as people with mental illness, people living with disabilities, older people, many of whom are living without support or adequate social services. I am thinking of the discrimination against Travellers, the suspicion of immigrants, asylum-seekers and refugees.

I am thinking also of the poverty of our planning, the huge inequality between our public and private services in health,

housing and transport. I am thinking too of the consumerism, exploitation, greed and ostentatious wealth that is in clear evidence. I
am thinking of drug abuse and alienation of young people. I am
thinking of the extreme individualism which drives out solidarity
and compassion and I am thinking of a comfortable mindset which
ignores or dismisses calls for inclusion and social justice as anti-
enterprise. And I am thinking too of those who have benefited economically but who have very little sense of the ethos and values on
which this State was founded and who do not have a sense of place
or a sense of belonging, whom society has failed civilly and spiritu-
ally and who have never been helped to see that they carry responsibility as citizens not only to make Ireland economically successful
but also to build a compassionate, caring community.

But there are, fortunately, people who are not happy with the
way society is going, even if they have benefited economically
themselves. We now have a society hungry to achieve its full potential and the challenge facing us is to discover ways in which all
our citizens can achieve their full potential and contribute to the
changes sweeping across Ireland and across the world. It is only
when this potential is unlocked for all that we will become a confident, successful, generous generation with a new conscience for
our time, a generation not content or comfortable until we are a
society that is all centre and no margins.

One of the greatest challenges we face is to break our fascination with what is ultimately a harmful and destructive idea of
what it is to be a human being — a view which sees us as solitary
beings forever pursuing our own individual good and purpose.
We are not lone nomads; we are part of a common humanity. We
are all in this together and for this reason we must seek the common good, restore the bonds of community, and replace our
fragmented society with a society that values the communal
rather than the individual.

This society is now in a position to decide the road it wants to
take, but to make this decision, we need to be able to imagine
what the society we want to build would be like, to articulate a
constructive view of that society, and to continue to create wealth

but to balance that wealth with greater social cohesion. We need to develop a humane form of society that is capable of replacing excessive individualism and consumerism with human values, a system capable not only of creating wealth but also of distributing it equitably.

To achieve this new economy of equity, we need to develop and articulate economic and social policies based on values that will ensure that the economy serves the people and not the other way around. We need a new kind of politics, which will be driven by moral principles and values rather than by the latest polls; which will think more about the needs and potential of the poor and vulnerable than about what suits the rich and powerful; and which will put more value on the pursuit of the common good than the demands of special interests. When we have agreed the values of this new society, then we need agreement on the objectives and actions to be taken in accordance with these values, and we need to establish performance indicators through which the actions and objectives can be examined and evaluated regularly in the light of the values, governed in an open, transparent and accountable manner.

There is a lacuna in this society which no organisation is addressing — namely the great unease, discontent, dissatisfaction, emptiness and sense of frustration that the relentless drive for economic growth and prosperity has brought in its trail. If we want to address this lacuna, we need the kind of leadership that will bring people of different traditions and backgrounds together around the values that unite us; leadership that will protect the human rights of every individual; leadership that will steer us through this current — if now slightly faltering — prosperity so that everyone gains from it and not just the few.

A society committed to the values of freedom, equality, solidarity, tolerance, respect for nature and shared responsibility sees responsible citizenship as twofold: not only is it a privilege, but it is also an opportunity to participate in building the life of society. In such a society, every voice matters, every vote counts, every act of responsible citizenship is an exercise of significant individual power. Such a society recognises that the human person is inherently social and so it is a society where families are supported and strengthened. Such a society recognises that every person, in addition to a right to life, has a right to food, shelter, health care, housing, education, employment — those things that are normal in that society and that allow them to participate fully in that society and live a decent life.

A society based on these values will ensure that the economy serves the people and not the other way around. In such a society, work is more than a means to a livelihood but is a form of continuing participation in the act of creation, a way of fulfilling each person's potential. Such a society recognises that the subordination of the human being to economic principles results from a distorted perception of reality.

A society based on these values will take positive steps to combat all forms of discrimination based on race, sex, ethnicity, religion or age because all forms of discrimination are seen as grave injustices and an affront to human dignity.

A society based on these values will promote responsible citizenship which ensures continuous participation in public life, where individuals bring their moral conviction to bear on civil tasks and choices, realising that protecting freedom and human rights are not only wise national priorities but are moral imperatives.

A society based on these values will ensure that every person possesses the basic dignity that comes not from any human quality or accomplishment, not from race or gender, age or economic status but from God.

A society based on these values will ensure that the public authorities have the common good as their prime responsibility. Every individual, no matter what their status, shares in promoting the welfare of community as well as a right to benefit from its welfare. Such a society will recognise that excluding any section of the population from participation in the life of the community, even at a minimal level, is a contradiction of its values and has to be rectified. Such a society will not be satisfied with only basic provision for the poor that simply prevents absolute poverty, but will also rectify the exclusion that comes from relative poverty, thus ensuring that everybody lives with dignity and with adequate resources and so can participate fully in society.

A society based on those values can never be run for the benefit of the rich but has to be run for the benefit of all. This society will ensure that nobody is marginalised and will bring back into their place in the community those who may have been marginalised in the past. In such a society, the existence of an alienated underclass, bereft of any sense of participation in or belonging to the wider community, will not be tolerated as a price worth paying in return for some other social advantage to be enjoyed by the majority.

A society based on these values ensures that environmental goods are not only available for careful use and enjoyment today but are held in trust for the use and enjoyment of future generations. In such a society, environmental goods could not be treated as having no intrinsic worth but merely elements in profit or loss. In such a society, the environment would be regarded as a great repository of natural wealth belonging to all humanity, present and future, freely and equally, and that each generation must take the natural environment on loan and must return it after use in as good condition as when it was first borrowed or better.

Such a society will protect the weakest in our midst and will overcome child poverty. It will be a society where parents can rear their children with respect for life, with a sense of hope and an ethic of stewardship and responsibility. Such a society will not accept or tolerate that the richest 10 per cent of our population is eleven times richer that the poorest 10 per cent, or that 20 per cent of households live on less than 50 per cent of the average wage and will seek to change it. It will be a society which will ensure that everybody has access to quality education, decent and affordable housing, affordable and accessible health care. It will be a society that will combat all prejudices and discrimination, overcoming all hostility towards asylum-seekers, immigrants, refugees, Travellers or any other group.

Such a society will pursue the values of justice and peace in a world where injustice is common, destitution is widespread and peace is too often destroyed by war and violence. It will address the tragedy that 35,000 children die every day as a result of hunger and lack of development around the world. Such a society is a one where every policy, practice and political platform will be measured on how they touch the human person — whether they enhance or diminish human life, dignity and human rights and how they advance the common good. Such a society will recognise that the human family extends across the globe and that each individual carries the responsibility to promote the common good in all parts of the world. Such a society will have a global ethic of fostering peaceful and stable relations among nations, responsible environmental policies and upholding human rights in the world community. It will work to overcome poverty in the poorest countries, which are shackled by debt, a burden that deprives them of the most basic essential services. It will play its role in helping to alleviate global poverty through foreign aid programmes for support and sustainable development, and it will participate in trade and other policies that protect human rights and environmental concerns. It will support the United Nations and other international bodies and international law so that these institutions become more effective, responsible for the addressing of global problems.

It will provide asylum and protection for all people fleeing persecution or who hold a well-founded fear of persecution in their homeland. It will provide a place of welcome on humanitarian grounds for vulnerable people seeking safety and economic, social and emotional security, giving special attention to unaccompanied women and children. It will provide an asylum process that is fair and speedy and that is trusted by those seeking it, not one designed to curb asylum-seekers, causing fear rather than trust and driving potential asylum-seekers underground to live as irregular migrants with no rights, subject to exploitation and leading to a system that benefits nobody.

It will develop a generous immigration policy, separate from its asylum policy, which protects immigrant workers from exploitation, promotes family reunification and safeguards the right of all persons to return to their homeland. It will not use immigrants as economic units but will treat them as human persons with huge potential and offering a positive contribution culturally, socially and economically to Irish society. It will extend to immigrants the full protection of the law, adequate health, welfare, education and housing service with fair and efficient processes and procedures. It will ensure that the gross inequalities are reduced, not exacerbated. It will be a society that is compassionate and fair towards immigrants and those seeking asylum and tough and harsh on the political, economic and social inequities at the root causes of migration and asylum.

If we take up this challenge to develop a society that is based on the values of freedom, equality, solidarity, tolerance, respect for nature and shared responsibility, we will not only become more cohesive and connected but set an example for the rest of the world.

2

BOSTON OR BERLIN?

Mary Banotti MEP

BOSTON VS BERLIN: WHICH OPTION FOR A JUST SOCIETY?

For many of my generation and my politics, the words "just society" have a particular meaning driven by Declan Costello's 1960s proposals for a radical social and political programme. As we came out of the difficult post-war period and the austerity, emigration and poverty which accompanied the 1950s, the Just Society approach emphasised the need for public policy to respond to the needs of all citizens and in particular the needs of those most vulnerable.

As a young woman, I was drawn to this vision and to the promise it held for our country and its citizens. I think many who became politicians were, and continue to be, motivated by such an ideal, although the actions of some have served to damage seriously the business of politics. However, the events of recent years, as tribunals unfold the stories of corruption, deceit and low (or even no) standards in, it seems, most high places, must cause us to challenge any assumptions that the phrase "just society" has or ever had a consistent meaning for us all. Indeed, it is interesting that so often in the litany of criticism, whether of political, church or business leaders, there is reference to the good things that they

did achieve. It is as though for many the ethical framework applied at some times and not others, to some actions but not to all.

The shock to our system of having to face the fact that many of
the supposedly strong strands of our social fabric are deeply
flawed offers an opportunity for the kind of reflection that is
needed if we are to take charge of where we go from here.

So what is a just society today? I particularly like the view of a
just society offered by Amartya Sen,[1] in the context of the developing world. Sen talks of how good government creates freedom,
which can come in many forms, and she suggests five central freedoms that are instrumental if people are to lead the lives that they
would like to lead. These are:

- *Political freedom*: choosing who governs and how they do so,
  and freedoms of communication such as speech and writing;

- *Economic freedom*: that people can produce, consume and ex-
  change, and that they have opportunities to do rewarding
  work;

- *Social opportunities*: in the provision of services such as health-
  care and education;

- *Transparency*: guarantees that citizens have access to clear and
  truthful information about current affairs and politics, and to
  the rights and services available to everybody;

- *Protective security*: against risks like unemployment, crime,
  famine or war.

Sen may be describing principles in the context of the developing
world but to my mind they are universal aspects of a just society.
Action is required not simply to ensure, but to sustain inclusion,
access and fair treatment for all, while at the same time creating
the optimum conditions for people to fulfill their potential.

Writer Robert Putnam makes a simple case for what I believe
to be the underpinnings in political terms of the Berlin model. In

---

[1] Sen, Amartya (1999), *Development as Freedom*, Oxford: Oxford University Press.

Making Democracy Work[2] he advocates the view that people who live together must co-operate if they are to achieve their best interests and that to achieve the common good we must take care not to privilege some groups over others. Fairness in how our institutions and processes work, and genuine access for all to those institutions and processes are also crucial to achieving the common good. In this lies a profound respect for the individual citizen throughout their life.

We need not look far to see how these principles have become blurred — if ever they were clear. In 2001, the Nice Referendum provided a neat example of how the elite in Ireland had begun to believe that theirs was the only view that mattered. Not only that, but their attitude to a fundamental element of our democracy — the overarching right of all citizens to determine the Constitution through referendums —confirmed what bordered on contempt.

A privileged group lost sight of the central role of the community of citizens, and in failing to communicate properly and with respect, denied them as voters access to a full understanding of the Treaty. It was no surprise to me that, faced with such obvious contempt, voters refused to do what they were told. In 2002, a far more considered, thorough approach to informing people, debating the issues and responding to concerns resulted in the Treaty being voted for favourably. Whether the initial sharp rebuke is adequate to ensure that in future Putnam's principles are kept at the centre of our democracy remains to be seen.

There are many examples that we could use to reflect on whether our democracy is working. The inequalities that exist in an area such as access to the law, for example, create an immediate imbalance which I do not believe is good for the country or the community. The evidence is that money buys a different legal service to that available to people without resources, instead of the system providing an equally rigorous service to all.

---

[2] Putnam, Robert D. et al. (1993), *Making Democracy Work: Civic Traditions in Modern Italy*, Princeton University Press.

Over the past three decades, many of the changes in legal rights in Ireland, particularly for those who are most vulnerable, have been driven from Europe and have been underpinned by commitments to a more egalitarian society and to balancing rights. In the Boston/Berlin debate the market is generally the starting point. The Boston model would have us construct the legal rights of workers, for example, in a minimalist way, believing that opportunity is there for all and that the individual needs only work hard and take advantage of opportunities, in order to succeed. In this scheme of things, that some fall by the wayside is a by-product of the individual's failings — capitalism, the market, is king.

But we are not simply a market. We are not the sum total of what we produce and what we consume. We do not start out with the same potential, and life does not deal us the same cards. Of course, economic growth and wealth are important but so too are other values. Those that forget this broader picture, and focus on profit and power at any cost and by any means, will come to grief. Look no further than Enron.

The Berlin model of frameworks of basic rights for workers has been crucial in establishing rights as diverse as setting minimum wage rates — the market is not king at any cost — to establishing European Works Councils that give workers voice in the decision-making that affects their companies. I believe that our economy and thus our wider society is served well by increasingly moving towards a balanced approach to the rights of workers and business.

In Ireland's rush to become an economic engine, it is perhaps not surprising that we became focused on having, and having now, and on an individualism that felt unconnected to community. It has been a fast and furious shift and gives us some indication of the need for an ethical and social framework to provide checks and balances — left to our own devices, perhaps, we have not the ethical sophistication to see this at close quarters.

The partnership process in Ireland has been one forum where the broad needs of the community are constantly presented, a reminder that the economic and social are always interconnected.

After fifteen years, the process is under strain, and not surprisingly. It would be far easier for the different interests to be the only, or one of just a few interests at the table. Partnership is in its infancy here and as long as the interest groups operate from different agendas of principle, fundamental tensions will exist. The tensions become more evident and the differences more influential at times of social and economic strain, such as we face now. For the process to grow, some profound and shared principles need to be in place and therein lies the challenge.

Are we more likely to find models that will help us in the US or in Europe? From my own experience, the US remains too focused on a market-driven perspective of society and an assumption that all things can flow from there. But for those near poverty in the US the situation is often extremely fragile. Redundancy, an accident or sudden illness, or simply growing older, can tip people into a spiral of poverty. There are few social supports for those with limited means.

Europe, on the other hand, continues to try to find more cohesive models which are designed to promote the well-being — wealth and health — of the whole society as well as the individuals, and the social responsibility that we share as we benefit from our individual rights. Some countries have tried harder than others — and have succeeded in part or for a time. The Nordic countries appear to have moved furthest in developing a civic appreciation, support and acceptance of the need for a just, *in every sense of the word*, society. In parts of Italy, the emphasis on high-quality social services and economic development have been mutually beneficial. For many years, the UK National Health Service was another model of a community-based approach to a fundamental aspect of justice — the right to health and health care. It too had the very widespread support of people who saw it in terms of the common good.

The "Berlin" model is work-in-progress but, to my mind, in the interests of our whole community will serve us far better than anything that "Boston" has to offer. However, that assumes that we all want the same thing and that we are prepared to work for and contribute to, as well as benefit from, a just society. It means that we audit carefully all aspects of our society — business, politics, civic society, the churches and so on, and that we measure up to those principles. It means that where we do not measure up, effective early warning systems kick in, identifying the problem and addressing the shortcomings.

In the absence of such early warning up to now, today we face a massive level of auditing of the failures of so many of the "pillars" of our a society. Through the media and various tribunals; the investigations of banking practice and non-resident accounts; the various blood-product related scandals; the exposure of the extent of child abuse and in particular the response of the Catholic Church and the State to this issue; we continue to be shocked and enraged. We have learned the hardest way possible that if we are not actively engaged in our community and wider society, if we do not demand transparency, then we cannot assume that what is done in our name is ethical or good.

A more community-rooted and balanced approach, as envisaged by the Berlin model, is to my mind the only healthy way forward. It is far from easy, demands more civic involvement and responsibility, makes explicit what we believe to be basic rights that should be enjoyed by all. It will not come about without far greater civic engagement and an appreciation of the nature of community and the interdependence of all people to protect and nourish the freedoms which are essential to democracy and a just society.

3

ETHICS AND THE DISTRIBUTION OF WEALTH

David Begg

IRELAND IN A GLOBAL SETTING

Any consideration of the distribution of wealth in Ireland from an ethical perspective must be located in the context of the global economic order now emerging. The reason for this is that Ireland, as a very open economy, is profoundly affected by globalisation. Indeed, we have been rated as the most globalised economy in the world. Globalisation is to a large extent a phenomenon of the type of capitalism which was associated with the United States. Ireland, of course, is heavily influenced by the US, being the recipient of twenty per cent of all Foreign Direct Investment (FDI) into Europe from that country.

Pope John Paul II published a social encyclical, *Centesimus Annus* on 1 May 1991. It was written to mark the centenary of *Rerum Novarum*, the original statement of the Catholic social teaching. *Centesimus Annus* contains a passage which presents a moral evaluation of capitalism in the following terms:

> Can it perhaps be said that, after the failure of Communism, capitalism is the victorious social system, and that capitalism should be the goal of the countries now making efforts to rebuild their economy and society? . . .

The answer is obviously complex. If by "capitalism" is meant an economic system which recognises the fundamental and positive role of business, the market, private property and the resulting responsibility for the means of production, as well as free human creativity in the economic sector, then the answer is certainly in the affirmative, even though it would perhaps be more appropriate to speak of a "business economy", "market economy", or simply "free economy". But if by "capitalism" is meant a system in which freedom in the economic sector is not circumscribed within a strong juridical framework which places it at the service of human freedom in its totality and sees it as a particular aspect of that freedom, the core of which is ethical and religious, then the reply is certainly negative.

This text was widely regarded as a challenge to the US model of capitalism.

A recently published book by Kevin Phillips called *Wealth and Democracy*[3] offers a more explicit critique of America. His thesis is that the US has moved away from being an economy which produces things towards one which exports its technologies to cheaper wage economies and instead substitutes for this an increasingly financialised economy in which banks, brokerage houses, investments and complex financial instruments dominate. This in turn has led to downward pressure on wages and living standards for ordinary workers.

The last two decades of the twentieth century saw an extraordinary concentration of American wealth in fewer and fewer hands. In 1981, the top one per cent of Americans "owned" 9.3 per cent of the economy; by 1997, they owned 15.8 per cent. In 1979, the top one per cent held a 20.5 per cent share of household wealth; by 1997, they held 40.1 per cent. In 1977, the top twenty

---

[3] Kevin Phillips (2002), *Wealth and Democracy*, Broadway Books, a division of Random House, New York.

per cent owned 44.2 per cent of all income in the US, but by 1999, that had jumped to 50.4 per cent.

The rich got measurably richer, particularly during the supposedly fair Clinton presidency, when all records were broken. The ratio of chief executives' pay to the hourly wages of ordinary workers soared from 93 times in 1988 to 419 in 1999. The average pay of the chief executives of the largest corporations rose by 481 per cent between 1990 and 1998 to an average of $10.6 million. Industrial wages barely kept pace with inflation. This makes something of a mockery of Plato's ideal, in what was admittedly, a smaller and simpler world, that no person should be worth more than four times another.

Ordinary Americans worked longer hours than their counterparts elsewhere. Whereas workers in Japan, Britain, Germany and France all worked fewer hours per annum in 1998 than they had in 1950, Americans worked longer. Apart from France, Britain, Canada and Japan, the entire world's industrial economies paid their workers more than America did. While the US gross domestic product more than doubled between 1959 and 1996, the Index of Social Health, which includes items such as child poverty and health care coverage, declined by 50 per cent.

While the experience in Ireland has been more benign, there is some basis for concerns at the trend of income distribution in the economy. The National Economic and Social Council (NESC)[4] has pointed out that the wage share of total gross value added fell by around seven per cent between 1991 and 1999. In terms of the distribution of wealth in society we are one of the most unequal countries in Europe and closer to the Anglo-American model. I will return to this point later.

The point Phillips tries to make in his conclusion is that the United States is perilously close to two potentially cataclysmic transformations: one is that the end of empire is near and the torch is about to be passed onto others, China being the favourite;

---

[4] "An Investment in Quality: Services, Inclusion and Enterprise", NESC No. 110, November 2002.

and the other is that the social strain caused by such vast inequalities will inevitably show itself, and arguably already has, in political and other forms of instability.

What makes this critique compelling is that Kevin Phillips is a Republican and former advisor to Richard Nixon.

THE SCANDALS OF CORPORATE AMERICA

The question of ethics arises here in two ways: is it ethical to have such inequality in society and to what extent is unethical behaviour at the root of the difficulties facing America, and by extension the global economy?

We are all now broadly aware of the scandals affecting corporate America and its satellites around the world. Apart from Enron itself, banks like JP Morgan Chase and Citigroup have been implicated. Three of the four largest auditing firms have been caught out, as have a variety of analysts and advisors. There have been scandals at Worldcom, AOL Time Warner, Adelphi Communications, ImClone, Tyco, Xerox and Dynergy. Household icons like Martha Stewart have been accused of insider trading. Jack "Neutron" Welch has been the latest heavy-hitter to fall into disrepute. His estranged wife revealed that General Electric was picking up the tab for wine, toiletries and sporting event tickets after his retirement. There will not be much sympathy for him amongst the GE workforce. During his term at the helm, he sacked 100,000 of them!

It is clear that in ethical terms, this is not just a question of a few rotten apples. The structure of the barrel itself is highly suspect and it will be hard to find anyone with clear enough hands to rectify it. Certainly it is unlikely to be the present political administration, as both the President and Vice President have their own problems of sloppy corporate governance with Harken Energy and Haliburton respectively.

In Ireland, of course, we were some years ahead of the Americans, with scandals going to the heart of the business/political nexus.

ETHICS IN THE MARKET PLACE

Business ethics is a study of moral standards and how these apply to the systems and organisations through which modern societies produce and distribute goods and services, and to the people who work within these organisations. Business ethics, in other words, is a form of applied ethics. It includes not only the analysis of moral norms and moral values, but also attempts to apply the conclusions of this analysis to that assortment of institutions, technologies, transactions, activities and pursuits that we call *business*.

As this description of business ethics suggests, the issues that business ethics covers encompass a wider variety of topics. A great deal has been written on the subject and efforts have been made to apply the philosophies of Kant, Adam Smith and Marx to the modern-day marketplace. The sheer scale and diversity of the modern transnational corporation makes this difficult.

At the beginning of the twenty-first century, General Motors, the world's largest automobile company, had revenues of €189 billion and employed more than 388,000 workers; Wal Mart, the world's largest retailer, had sales of €165 billion and 1,140,000 employees; General Electric, the world's largest maker of electrical equipment, had sales of €111 billion and 340,000 employees. Of the world's 190 nations, only a handful (Canada, France, Germany, Italy, Japan, United States, Russia, United Kingdom) had government budgets larger than any one of these company's sales revenues, and most of the world's nations had fewer workers engaged in their entire auto, retailing, electrical, or computer industries than did these gigantic companies. About half of America's combined industrial profits and earnings are in the hands of about 100 such large corporations, each of which has assets worth over €1 billion.

The fact that multinationals operate in more than one country produces ethical dilemmas for their managers which firms limited to a single country do not face. First, because the multinational has operations in more than one country, it has the ability to shift its operations out of any country that becomes inhospitable and relocate in another country that offers it cheaper labour, less stringent laws or more favourable treatment. This ability to shift its operations sometimes enables the multinational to escape the social controls that a single nation might attempt to impose on the multinational and can allow the multinational to pit one country against another. Environmental laws, for example, which can ensure that domestic companies operate in the responsible manner that a country deems right for its people, may not be effective constraints on a multinational that can simply move or threaten to move to a country without such laws. Again, union rules that can ensure fair treatment of workers or decent wages may be ineffective against a multinational that can go or threaten to go anywhere in the world to look for cheap labour.

The resistance to the inclusion of protocols relating to labour standards in World Trade Organisation agreements is instructive. This is often portrayed as an attempt at protectionism by Western trade unions but it is not. Neither is it a demand that wage rates in developing countries should be the same as in industrialised countries. What is being sought is the right of workers in poor countries to organise and to bargain collectively with employers and to also eliminate inappropriate child labour. It is then for the workers to decide what they can advocate for in their particular circumstances without damaging their capacity to trade. The naked use of power and influence to prevent any progress on core labour standards is an example of the enduring struggle between capital and labour and an example of the ethical indifference of the former.

THE ETHICAL FAILURE OF GLOBALISATION

Continuing this theme, it is interesting to note that the large corporations, or at least some of them, put some effort into trying to convince the public that they act in an ethical way. If you tune in to BBC World Television for "World Business Report" in the morning you will see many advertisements purporting to demonstrate good corporate citizenship in action. Mainly these are based on respect for the environment and how oil companies, for example, concern themselves with doing no harm. However, corporate support for addressing environmental issues in a cohesive way is suspect to say the least. The US Government, under the influence of its business supporters, has effectively rejected the Kyoto Agreement. In justice, it must be said that there are exceptions to this generalisation. In 1987, Merck developed a drug called Mectizan which can cure river blindness, a particularly horrible disease prevalent in Africa. They gave it away virtually free of charge to those countries most affected by the disease. Nevertheless, it is depressing that the fruits of a global economy worth $30 trillion are so unequally distributed.

The statistics on poverty are depressing. Over one and a half billion people live on less than one US dollar per day. There are 815 million undernourished people in the world; 777 million of them in developing countries, 27 million in transitional economies and 11 million in industrialised countries. Every 3.6 seconds, someone dies of hunger. Yet there is plenty of food in the world for everyone to have over twice the daily calorific intake they need. There are 34 million people suffering from HIV/AIDS, most of them in sub-Saharan Africa.

Transnational Corporations (TNCs) account for 70 per cent of global trade, with four companies accounting for about 90 per cent of exports of corn, wheat, coffee, tea and pineapples. The top five agro-chemical companies control almost the entire global genetically modified seed market. While an estimated 30,000 plant species have edible parts, just three — wheat, rice and maize — supply more than half the world's food. As these staples are genetically engineered and patented, the power wielded by TNCs in the global food supply will tighten. Small-scale farmers and local co-operatives in developing countries are expected to compete, on a very uneven playing field, against corporations and heavily subsidised developed country farmers. In 1999, OECD countries spent €361 billion subsidising agriculture. This figure is seven times global official development assistance, which amounted to about €50 billion in the same year.

The model of capitalism, shaped by a very conservative American doctrine, which is the driving force behind globalisation, can hardly be considered ethical on the basis of this evidence.

ETHICS AND THE DISTRIBUTION OF WEALTH IN IRELAND

In terms of the distribution of wealth, Ireland is closer to the Anglo-American model than to the more socially inclusive European model.

The objective of the Congress of Trade Unions in entering the Programme for National Recovery in 1987 was to transform Ireland into a modern European country in both economic and social terms and to do so by replacing our inherited British model of confrontational industrial relations with one more akin to the partnership approach of the Germans, Scandinavians and Dutch.

The economic transformation of Ireland was achieved. By subsidising wages (and profits) from the Exchequer through tax reduction and securing stable industrial relations, the conditions for economic growth were established. The proportion of wealth taken by profits increased, which in turn attracted Foreign Direct Investment. Investment created economic growth and jobs which, in turn, reduced dependency and improved the public finances.

At first sight, this was a virtuous circle but it was an incomplete circle. Economic growth has boosted GDP per capita to 112 per cent of the EU average. A major social objective of full employment was also achieved. However, we are far behind Europe in terms of social development and supporting infrastructure. For instance:

- The wealth of the nation is not fairly distributed either geographically or to socio-economic groupings. In fact, next to Portugal, we are the most unequal society in Europe;

- Health care is widely accepted as inadequate;

- Housing is in crisis. One third of young people have to make a choice between having a family or buying a house. There are 54,000 people on the social housing waiting list;

- The cost of housing has forced people to live in provincial towns like Mullingar and Dundalk even though they may work in Dublin;

- Increasing female labour force participation is, in turn, increasing demand for childcare but this is either not sufficiently available or very expensive.

This is not meant to be an exhaustive list of social deficits; but even these examples do carry a heavy price tag.

The displacement of the Dublin region's population growth to locations 30 to 50 miles away from the city is a particularly disturbing phenomenon, which has both adverse economic and social implications. Commuter transport from such distant points — whether by car or by public transport — will impose increased economic and environmental costs on the community as a whole because of the need to provide additional roads and public transport. There are, moreover, unquantifiable but very serious human and social costs involved in long-distance commuting, for it greatly reduces the amount of time parents can spend with their children.

High levels of indebtedness, transport costs and childcare needs feed into wage demands. Ireland is already the most expensive country in Europe according to Forfás — we have the most expensive potatoes, eggs, chickens and antibiotics. It is the most expensive place also to smoke or drink, to buy a cup of coffee or a hamburger.

In summary, the history of the last fifteen years is that the unions made a bargain with employers and government to achieve economic growth sufficient to create full employment. It was the right thing to do at the time, even though it disproportionately benefited business. The bargain now has to be re-engineered to achieve a comparable level of social development.

It seems to me that if we want to achieve economic *and* social development comparable with the more advanced European nations, we will have to be willing in general terms to invest what those counties invest. I recognise that our demographics give us an advantage in terms of pensions expenditure but, realistically, if it costs on average 47.5 per cent of GDP to provide public services in Europe, I do not see how we can get the same quality services for 30 per cent of GDP. As a people, we have to adopt a more realistic perspective on the link between taxation and public services. We cannot continue to believe that we can simultaneously lower taxes and improve public services.

We have come to believe too much, perhaps, in the premise that our dependence on Foreign Direct Investment leaves us with limited choices as to how we manage our domestic economy. I do not believe this to be the case. Globalisation may be dominated by a neo-liberal agenda, but significant room for political action and national development strategies remain.

I contend that the major threats to the sustainability of the Irish development model, as it has matured over the past fifteen years, arises not so much from our dependency on investment but rather from the possibility of rising inequality undermining the socio-political compromises which allowed economic growth to happen. The creation of an indigenous manufacturing and information industry complex that is not directly dependent on transnational corporations has lessened our dependence on FDI somewhat.

Furthermore, this indigenous base has very deep roots in the local economy and society and has significantly upgraded its technical and business capabilities. The real threat to sustainability, therefore, is likely to be the lack of social solidarity reflected in, and exacerbated by, increasing income inequality — not dependence on foreign capital. However, there are significant actions that can be taken at the national level to ameliorate this inequality precisely because foreign investment does not dominate the economy as totally as it once did. The legitimate critique of the over-reliance on foreign investment may, if taken too far, result in letting domestic elites off the hook. The tendency of recent tax and other fiscal decisions to increase inequality has little or nothing to do with the desire to attract further foreign investment.

We really do have to consider whether, at some point, we will reach the status of a mature industrial society capable of sustaining high quality public services with a tax policy to facilitate this. Specifically, do we need to apply a corporation tax rate of 12.5 per cent to hotels and banks in circumstances where we are struggling with such social service deficits by comparison with the rest of the European Union? The European Union spends 47.5 per cent of its GDP on average on these objectives while our spend is around 33 per cent. If we are to increase expenditure we have to increase tax and our problem here is that we have a very narrow tax base. As it is, a disproportionately high burden falls to income and indirect taxes.

The Netherlands is a country which seems to have achieved a comparable level of economic growth without compromising the ethical basis of wealth distribution in society. One of the most successful economies in Europe in the 1990s, it attracted a lot of foreign investment. It revitalised its national partnership institutions and achieved a strong growth dynamic without increasing inequality. This suggests that there are likely to be more egalitarian, yet successful, globalisation models than those pursued by Ireland. It is to such models that we must now turn to if we are to complete the transformation of Ireland into a country which combines economic efficiency, individual freedom and social justice in an ethical balance which is ultimately sustainable. In the words of the former French Prime Minister, Lionel Jospin: "We need a market economy but not a market society."

4

BUSINESS ETHICS IN A FREE MARKET

Martin O'Donoghue

BEING GOOD IS GOOD BUSINESS

In Plato's *Republic*, the discussion of Justice is rounded off by Socrates concluding that Justice consists in "each doing their own task and not meddling in the tasks of others".

The task of a business firm operating in a free competitive economy is to make a profit from its activities. Leaving aside chance accidents or other unwanted events, it is more likely to succeed by acting ethically. There is no inherent conflict between making profits and acting in the public interest.

This may surprise some, given the recent wave of business scandals in Ireland and elsewhere, which leads to the impression that there is something antisocial or unjust in business behaviour. Common-sense observation, however, shows why acting ethically makes good business sense. Every day, millions of people buy and sell things, they give their money to banks, they pay in advance for a future holiday or other services — all done with people they do not know. They are willing to act like this because they *trust* that the person or firm with whom they are dealing will *honour* their side of the bargain. We are confident that banks will safeguard our money, the shop will not supply bad or faulty goods, or the holiday firm will provide the agreed services when the time comes.

It is easy to see why a good reputation will help business success. The tailor who makes excellent clothes, the carrier who delivers on time, the shop which always supplies quality goods and promptly replaces any that are shown to be faulty, are far more likely to thrive by comparison with their competitors who acquire uncertain or unreliable reputations.

So business firms that do their own task well are behaving justly, in the Socratic sense. And there are other ethically positive features about firms in a competitive market system. All buyers and sellers are treated equally; there is no discrimination since everybody is free to decide for themselves what transactions they wish to undertake, within their ability to pay.

The profits made by firms in this competitive system are also ethically superior because they represent a more efficient use of the resources available to them, whereas firms who use resources in wasteful or incompetent ways make losses and fail their *moral* responsibility to use scarce resources productively. (In the Gospel story of the talents, it is the servant who neglects to use the money he was given who behaved unjustly.)

A free competitive market system also played an important role in the development of political democracy. The growth of market trading led to the development of a system of commercial law — establishing the rights and obligations attached to contracts, the entitlements to ownership of goods or property, and to procedures for resolving disputes. In this commercial legal framework, people are treated equally and their rights are based on the merits of the transaction and on their behaviour. This was in contrast to the prevailing political system, which conferred different rights to different social classes, such as aristocrats, commoners or serfs, based on the *power* they possessed.

The importance of having a proper democratic system of commercial law and business can be seen from the experience of the former Soviet Union. Instead of the former state firms being transferred to widespread democratic shareholding by the people, the ownership of many huge enterprises ended up in the hands of a few. The ability to transact business successfully can depend far more on having powerful friends and adequate protection, rather than attempting to rely on legal contracts. This tendency for business behaviour to pay little attention to western ethical standards and to rely more on the exercise of power, is hardly surprising in a society which replaced an earlier system of hierarchical power under the Tsars with an equally oppressive undemocratic communist system.

BUT ALL IS NOT PERFECT

While western firms can be profitable as well as being just, egalitarian and democratic, this does not apply in all cases. As with all human endeavours, there is no perfection, so that firms may behave and make profits for reasons which do not satisfy our ethical criteria.

One important influence in practice is the amount of relevant information which people possess. In earlier times, most people lived out their lives within a small geographical area, having little contact with the outside world. Living standards were simple, transactions fewer in number and conditions tended to change slowly. In such a world, it was possible to be reasonably well informed about the merits of traders and their wares. Today, it is almost impossible for the average person to compare the merits of the constantly changing flow of products and services available. So information becomes valuable and firms find that the public perception of a firm can be more influential in its success than the actual merits of its products. Advertising, which initially may have been used simply to inform people about the firm and its products, now becomes a vehicle for influencing their buying behaviour (Packard's "hidden persuaders").

The ability to influence a firm's performance, whether by advertising or other means, marks a crucially important difference from the competitive norm, because it introduces *power* into market behaviour, whereas a defining feature for a competitive situation is the absence of power by any buyer or seller to influence the outcome.

As modern economies evolved into larger-scale, more complex entities, market power became a continuing feature, giving rise in some cases to outright monopoly (where one firm controls demand or supply) or more usually to monopolistic markets (where a small number of firms can exercise significant influence). In such circumstances, it is possible for firms to make "unjust" profits through abuse of the power which they possess. This gives rise for the need to develop appropriate additions to the system of commercial law in order to regulate the behaviour of firms in such markets. Part of European Union (EU) law, for example, deals with issues such as the abuse of dominant positions and regulation of restrictive practices by firms.

It is relevant to add, however, that this more complex modern legal system also provides for the creation of monopoly-type situations — the patent laws being one common example. A great deal of time, money and other resources may go into the development of some new product, and in order to give the inventors an opportunity to recover these costs, they are granted patent or copyright protection for a number of years, to prevent any other firms from copying their original invention. This system gives rise to many disputes as to what is "fair" or "just"; this is usually cast in the form of a debate between the "private" and the "public" good. Theoretically, once the new knowledge has been produced, the maximum social benefits are likely to be derived by making this knowledge available free to everybody else. However, were this to be done, it would not pay the private firms to incur the research and development (R&D) costs necessary to make the new discovery. A contemporary example of this form of dispute arises with the introduction of new drugs. The high initial prices are set to recover the R&D costs as well as the actual cost of producing the drug. The argument is made that poor countries should be able to have free access to this knowledge, so as to have these drugs more cheaply.

Another feature of modern economies which moves us further away from the initial competitive market illustration is the emergence of another legal creation — the limited company, which acquires a legal personality of its own. As modern industries became larger in scale, it became increasingly too expensive or risky for any one person or group of partners to invest the large sums of money needed. The formation of a limited company (as the name implies), means that any one person's involvement or risk is limited to the amount of their shareholding in the firm. In this way, people avoid the risk of being bankrupted and losing all of their assets should the firm fail.

While the limited company has been of enormous economic benefit in facilitating the creation of countless firms, it also gives rise to fresh ethical dangers. There is now a separation between the legal owners of a firm (the shareholders) and the managers and staff who actually run the firm on a daily basis. While the objective of the firm remains unchanged (to make a profit), this is a less relevant objective for the managers and staff. Also, while attempts can be, and are, made to overcome this divergence of interests by having profit-sharing schemes, the gap between ownership and control opens up the scope for difficulties.

The purpose in drawing attention to these deviations from the original competitive illustration is to show the basis for the problems and scandals that beset modern business. The one further imperfection, which has been present in all ages up to the present, has been human frailties and weaknesses. The temptation to cheat has been present in all systems.

The trader who can give short measure, the tailor who can use poorer cloth, the publican who can water the whiskey — all can make bigger profits, provided they are not found out. Even if only small differences in weight or quality occur, and only very few traders ever cheat, then there is a good chance they may succeed. Temptation being what it is, no class was blameless — history offers many examples of kings and rulers cheating on the gold or silver in their coins. These unjust profits are only feasible because the bulk of trading is honest — in effect, the cheats get a "free bonus" from the honesty of others. In Groucho Marx's terms, "if you can fake sincerity you have it made".

IS MODERN CHEATING OR CORRUPTION ANY DIFFERENT TO THE OLD?

In the sense that cheating is always cheating, the answer to this question would be "no"; but in terms of its scale and nature, and especially in its consequences and the responses to it, the answer is "yes".

In earlier, simpler societies, the distinction between the trading classes and the aristocratic or other ruling classes was much sharper — aristocrats, for example, were specifically prohibited from engaging in commerce. For traders, their word was their bond, and cheating meant disgrace. Rulers could exercise power, behave more arbitrarily, demand service and loyalty from their subjects, and in general, relationships between classes were hierarchical. (For convenience, these are labelled "political" characteristics.) A large modern business on the other hand presents a confusing mixture of both systems. To the extent that it is buying and selling, it must appear to be fair and trustworthy in its dealing. But if the public perception is based on persuasive publicity or accepted brand names for its products, and given the separation between ownership and control, then the scope exists for unjust practices to develop.

Success for the management and staff may come to be viewed in terms of making the firm bigger. Bigger size can lead to more market power, making it easier to manage and control, and more growth usually means more jobs and promotion opportunities for staff. The large staff numbers require more hierarchical internal management structures. There tends to be a focus on loyalty to colleagues because all will share in the success of the firm.

This blend of the trading and political characteristics can produce positive benefits if all are behaving honestly, but it can result in serious costs when any wrongdoing occurs. If staff in some areas behave wrongly, their colleagues may be reluctant to take any action from a sense of loyalty (as the treatment given to most "whistleblowers" demonstrates). This is just as likely to apply at both the most senior and junior staff levels.

INSTITUTIONAL WRONGDOING

In addition to this institutional aspect, there appears to be a tendency to accept or condone business wrongdoing more readily nowadays than in earlier times. This does not seem to be the result of any single factor, but is rather due to the overall effect of various changes in attitudes and behaviour.

Until recently, the majority of Irish people came from a rural environment, and most commercial, social and other activity would primarily be with friends and neighbours rather than with strangers. In the move to more dispersed urban-based living, there would be a tendency to retain links based on local culture (affinity with people from the same town or county). Applying these values to business dealings is popular (giving a discount or special deal to someone from the home town, giving a job to the former neighbour's child). This may make good business sense — there is a better chance of knowing how competent our neighbours are — but it also helps to create the environment in which discrimination can arise, because now all buyers or sellers are not treated equally — as our competitive system would expect.

A second influence was the shift in moral attitudes, perhaps best illustrated by the case of taxation. The growth in the scale of government activities over the past decades called for greatly increased levels of taxation to finance them. Heavy taxes can cause difficulties in many cases, and not surprisingly, led many people to avoid some or all of them if possible. And if those troubled in conscience sought priestly advice, this generally took the attitude that the moral obligation was to pay one's fair share of tax, but not an excessive or unjust amount. Hardly surprising that an active industry should have developed for devising tax avoidance.

A third influence was ideology. In the political sphere, the gradual emergence of more broadly based democratic types of government was accompanied by other changes in social relations, especially the relationships between employers and workers.

One of the most influential nineteenth-century theories was that of Marx. In his system, firms make their profits by "exploiting" their workers. Earlier Christian-based concepts of each using their respective talents to contribute to their common goal of earning a just living from their business, and with their behaviour governed by norms such as "just price" and "just wage", are replaced in the Marxian world with a perpetual struggle between employer and worker. All profits were unearned and unjust, and the workers' share depended on their power. Organised trade unions became an instrument for acquiring the necessary bargaining power.

The twentieth-century development of so many large-scale businesses created situations where instead of the Marxian conflict, management and workers use their combined power to sustain higher prices and wages at the expense of their customers.

The modern outcome is thus one which removes any sense of legitimacy from such profits and also ironically one where workers become party to this "exploitation". While the theoretical basis for Marx's concept of "exploitation" has long been discarded as erroneous and outmoded, it still permeates the thinking of many left-wing groups.

Overall, the combination of institutional, social, cultural, moral and ideological changes over the decades have led to a great deal of confusion and misunderstanding on the proper role and responsibilities of business, and on their proper relationships with other elements of society.

HONEST BUSINESS

The essential features of healthy business activity remain unchanged. It is still essential that business dealings are founded on trust and honesty. It is still necessary that they should make sufficient profits to both sustain existing activities and also provide the incentive for future innovation.

What has changed is the growth of *power* in modern business activities both within and between firms. Because of the nature and size of many modern businesses, this cannot be completely avoided. But the effects are, first, that profits levels may be excessive (abuse of a dominant position in a market); secondly, there may be discrimination (not all buyers or sellers treated equally); and thirdly, they may be less democratic (lack of freedom for new entrants — "closed shops" for workers, patent laws for firms).

To state that these features of many modern businesses do not meet those of firms in free competitive markets is not automatically to assume that their behaviour is wrong or their profits unjustified. The case of patent laws is an example where the law deliberately discriminates in order to achieve what it deems the best available result in an imperfect world.

What it does mean is that a sufficient set of rules, supervision, and penalties for wrongdoing must be in place to ensure that abuses are not condoned and that wrongdoing is punished.

THE ROLE OF THE GUARDIANS

In Plato's *Republic*, the task of dealing with wrongdoing and seeing that justice was done was entrusted to the Guardians.

In our societies, this work is undertaken by governments and the courts, with much of the detailed supervision for specific areas such as business carried out by government departments or specialised agencies.

The main elements of a supervisory system follow logically from the discussion above:

- To promote free competition where possible and to establish an appropriate code of regulation and supervision where it is not.

- To emphasise openness and accountability for all sectors.

- To abolish self-regulation of industries or professional bodies.

- To give greater support and encouragement for "whistleblowers" who report wrongdoing in their organisations.

- To have speedy and effective enforcement of laws and codes of conduct, to demonstrate that crime will not pay.

Were these things done, there could be greater confidence in allowing business to get on "with doing its own task". What has been lacking to date is that others have not been "doing their tasks" well. Law enforcement has been slow and often nonexistent. Outdated systems and codes of behaviour have been allowed to continue. There has been confusion by people applying the more flexible, tolerant discriminatory patterns of conduct relevant in family or social life to business situations which require more predictable, universally valid codes, with the result that wrongdoing can occur because it is not recognised as being wrong.

So the final requirement for a healthy republic, as with Plato, is to educate and inform people of the reasons why all forms of cheating, wrongdoing and corruption in business life must be opposed and punished, because their spread would ultimately destroy not only business, but democracy itself.

5

ETHICS, COMPETITION AND PROFIT: A BUSINESS PERSPECTIVE

Feargal Quinn

One of the problems that people in business in Ireland face is the general public attitude to their activities. This attitude, however well-intentioned, is not supportive of ethical behaviour in business.

Let me approach this in a somewhat roundabout way. If I talk about the history of my company, I am telling the story of a tiny enterprise that began over forty years ago in Dundalk with a mere handful of colleagues and which has now grown to a point where our team numbers nearly 6,000 at nineteen locations around the country.

It is a story of the kind we would all like to see more of, so it is appropriate to ask: what is the one *essential* ingredient of this progress?

- A novel approach?
- An entrepreneurial spirit?
- A dedication to customer service?

If I propose any of those factors to an Irish audience, I will have many heads nodding in agreement. But, though all have been critical to Superquinn's progress, none of these is the one that is essential to any successful business.

That essential factor is . . . *profit*.

And that word is enough to set the lips curling in disdain. All of a sudden, the "good guy" has introduced a disreputable concept that, to very many people in Ireland, is regarded as inherently bad.

Profit is seen, at best, as a necessary evil. Unlike in other cultures, it is not part of our conventional wisdom in Ireland to regard profit as a necessary *good*. We are slow to see it as the one essential element in making an economy grow, essential because only from profit can come the resources to provide the investment that will inevitably be needed to fund growth.

To show how deeply this is ingrained in the Irish psyche, let us look no further than the statutes establishing our commercial semi-state bodies. Invariably in such legislation, you will find a clause that imposes on the body the obligation "to break even, taking one year with another". The implication is that breaking even is enough to ensure continued success, and that the correct posture for a State company is to be not-for-profit.

That implication is not only wrong; it is dangerously wrong. Many of the problems that our commercial semi-state bodies have run into in recent years have occurred precisely because they have not been able to generate the resources they needed for investment — in other words, because they were not making enough profit to fund their growth.

To survive, let alone to grow, every business needs a constant flow of new investment. Profit, far from being an undesirable aspect of business activity, is as desirable and necessary as any other business cost. Profit, properly regarded, is a cost of doing business in the future.

Why do negative attitudes to profit matter? And why is it, as I claimed at the beginning, unsupportive of ethical behaviour by people in business?

It matters because of what it implies. If profit is in itself undesirable, those who engage in the business of making a profit are outside the pale from the start. The attitude encourages people to believe that by getting involved in business at all, they have crossed some kind of ethical divide. Once they have crossed that divide, the only questions that arise are ones of degree.

So if we wish to raise the ethical standards in Irish business, the first thing we need to do is redraw our moral map. The ethical issues arising from profit are not due to its existence, but to its misuse.

Profits *can* be excessive.

Profits *can* be unfair, they *can* be exploitative.

We need both legal and moral restraints against such activities. But we do not help to control or discourage them by starting from the viewpoint that all profit is inherently bad, like greed. Greed *is* inherently bad, but all profit is not greed.

How, then, do we control excessive or unfair profits? In my view, the most effective way is through competition. Competition is what ensures a moral balance between buyer and seller.

In the absence of competition, the only choice a buyer has is between buying and not buying. But in the real world, the choice of not buying at all is seldom a realistic one. If one provider of goods or services has a monopoly, there is no restraint on the resultant profit — and, incidentally, no incentive at all to behave in the interests of the buyer.

On the other hand, where the buyer has a free choice between genuinely competing suppliers, there is an automatic constraint against excessive profits and an inbuilt incentive to suppliers to grow their business through meeting their customers' needs.

Competition is what keeps people in business honest; competition is what contains their greed. (No wonder they don't like it!)

We would, in my view, make a major leap forward if we moved our ethical goalposts away from "profit is inherently bad" and pitched them in a different position: "competition is inherently good". The fact that we have been so slow to do this is reflected in the fact that it is only recently that we have developed a legal system for regulating competition, and then only under pressure from Europe rather than out of any philosophical convictions.

Another aspect of the way we look at things could be seen in the various debates about privatisation that have taken place over the past decade. A great deal of ideological heat was generated as to the appropriateness of State ownership or private ownership of an enterprise. But very little attention was given to what to my mind was the real issue — and which unlike the ownership question did have a moral dimension — namely, what arrangement will foster the most competition?

A third insight into how we tend to think on this matter was reflected in the debates in the late 1990s that led to the setting up of the regulator's office for telecommunications, which was made necessary by the introduction of competition into that sector. The legislation conceived the regulator as simply a fair arbitrator between whatever competitors entered the market; I, on the other hand, argued that the public good required a regulator whose task would include the active *encouragement* of competition. I didn't win that argument at the time, but I think events since have proved me right.

However, shifting the goalposts to make competition our central concern is not the end of the matter. Rather, it is a proper positioning for a debate which must be ongoing, and which to be complete needs a moral dimension as well as a purely legal one.

Let me illustrate this by considering the concept of "fair competition". It goes without saying that fairness in competition is both necessary and desirable. But fairness is not something that can always be considered in a totally self-contained way, or by criteria that can be defined solely in legal terms.

Suppose, to take an example from my own industry, you allow the development of retail outlets so huge that to be viable they have to serve entire regions, and as a consequence make unviable any smaller outlets in towns and villages across the region.

In the narrow sense, such competition is "fair". But in the wider sense of the public good, does it make sense to undermine completely the traditional social geography of our country?

Before you say "no", however, remember that, in its essentials, this is the same argument that has always been put forward to oppose any kind of development that threatened the viability of an existing business. If we always had said "no" to this, Ireland today would have no supermarkets and be served exclusively by corner shops.

My point here is not to argue that "yes" or "no" is always the right response, but rather that the right response can change with the circumstances of each case — and should be decided, in the final analysis, on the basis of our values and our view as to what kind of a community we wish to create.

We should not look to a legal system to insulate us from this kind of moral debate. Neither should we dismiss the issue as beneath our notice because it may be presented as exclusively a business issue. Though it certainly is a business issue in that profits and losses are involved for some of the players, it is a public issue in that what we decide has wide and long-lasting ramifications for the way in which almost everybody lives their lives.

If embracing competition as a central good does not excuse us from the responsibility of considering the decisions it entails, neither should we be blind to the ethical dilemmas that competition can create as a side-effect.

One of the most fundamental choices available to us in life is that of choosing our friends, our acquaintances or who we do business with. By and large, we tend to choose our friends, acquaintances, or business associates from those with whom we are in broad agreement on things we consider important. At an individual level, we (rightly, in my view) treasure the freedom *not* to do business with a person or company with which we have a fundamental moral disagreement.

One of the side-effects of a competitive economy is that companies serving the public do not have the same freedom to choose who they do business with. The reason is very simple: if they exercised that freedom, they would usually go out of business very quickly indeed.

This has been a very real issue for me throughout most of my business life. In the nature of things, a business like mine sells thousands of individual goods, sourced from all parts of the world. Ethical issues arise all the time, either with the regime of the country they come from (South Africa, Israel, Chile, Colombia, etc.) or with production practices (slave labour, child labour, prices that exploit the original producer, use of chemicals or genetic engineering with unknown potential consequences, disregard for the environment, etc.), or even with the nature of the product itself (alcohol, cigarettes, etc.). The list goes on and on. Since going into business I can hardly remember a single month going by without our being asked by somebody, either an individual customer or an organisation, *not* to sell a particular product for ethical reasons. Very early on I realised that, however much I might sympathise with the particular cause involved, to apply a boycott at our level would be commercially disastrous.

The reality was that, in each case, the customers concerned with any particular issue were always in a minority — sometimes a tiny minority. Most customers were indifferent to the issue, but usually clear in their wish to go on buying the goods concerned.

So the dilemma presented to us was between being "morally blind" in our buying decisions or refusing to sell to the majority of customers goods they wanted to buy — and which if they did not buy from us they would get from our competitors. Anyone who has done business in a competitive environment will realise that you survive by giving your customers reasons to do business with you, not by giving them reasons to go to your competitors instead.

But, to take this argument to a further level, suppose a smart lobby group attacks this on an industry-wide level, and manages to get all retailers to agree not to stock a particular product? Would this not nullify the competition argument? Yes, but then the ground shifts to the question of how much support the lobby group has. If an overwhelming majority of customers agree with the boycott, well and good. But if even a significant minority of customers want to buy the goods, then I believe they should have the freedom to do so.

I think in ethical terms it comes down to this: the individual freedom to buy or not to buy is one thing; removing that freedom from other people is something quite different. For me, the lesser evil is sometimes selling goods that have a morally doubtful whiff about them.

In this respect, an individual retailer is in quite a different position to that of a government restricting sales for safety or health reasons — I believe government has the right, and indeed the duty, to protect its citizens from known hazards.

This is not, however, to say that players in the distribution chain do not have a role to play in influencing their suppliers. Because of where they are placed in the chain, they are often better positioned than an individual customer to relay the concerns that customers have to the ultimate producers — and in my view, we have a clear duty to do so.

There have been some notable successes in this regard, as well as some unforeseen negative side-effects. For instance, pressure was successfully put on Bangladeshi textile producers to stop employing child labour. Unfortunately, nobody thought to ensure that the children thrown out of work would be looked after — in a country that lacks universal free schooling and where the children's earnings were often critical to their whole family's survival. When we take action of this kind, we surely have an obligation to think all the implications through and take responsibility for the knock-on effects.

In general, though, it may surprise some people to find that I tend to be a little wary of any business scenario that casts companies in the role of "do-gooders". In recent years, in pursuit of the public relations objective of establishing an image as a "good corporate citizen", many companies have chosen to make sizeable financial contributions to various community, artistic or charitable causes.

My own experience is that, very often, a company's customers see such generosity as the self-interested activity it usually is. Even more sharply, many customers have often expressed to me the view that they resent "their money" being spent by us in this way. "Give us lower prices and let us spend the savings in whatever way we choose" is a common sentiment.

On the other hand, win-win opportunities do arise for business companies, and I believe we should focus our attention more on them. For instance, while *not* selling particular products is fraught with the problems I have outlined above, making a positive decision to stock a particular product can often have very beneficial results.

From the beginning, my company made a definite policy of offering customers the choice of buying an Irish product, where such was available; we saw that as part of our basic obligation to the community we do business in. Again, choosing to offer our customers "fair trade coffee" is a positive way of addressing the ethical conundrums of the world coffee market.

Because I have chosen to highlight what I see as the neglected area of competition as a central public good, I have left it to now to turn my attention to what is undoubtedly the classic "occasion of sin" in business ethics — conflict of interest.

Most ethical problems in business can be seen as conflicts of interest, and most of them (such as, for example, simple fraud or theft) apply equally in communities anywhere in the world. But the nature and history of our society in Ireland presents us with a number of special issues:

- Where publicly owned companies are concerned, the problems to do with insider trading become quite intense in a community as small and as tightly-knit as ours.

  This would seem to call for a greater standard of vigilance by comparison with other countries, rather than settling for a diluted form of control.

- Our late development has brought us suddenly, and without previous experience, to the task of sharing out scarce resources among a necessarily limited number of beneficiaries — whether these resources are planning permissions in the property area or licences to operate restricted monopolies in the area of public utilities.

What I think we have to learn from our experience so far is that altogether new and more demanding standards of public openness and accountability must be developed if we are not to slide into a society where corruption becomes endemic.

- Because today, and especially in Ireland, so much of business activity is entwined with that of government, the way we govern ourselves as a nation also needs to be much more open and accountable than before.

That means, for instance, bringing our parliament back to the centre of affairs, from the sidelines to which it has been banished increasingly over the past two decades. There is a widespread perception today that government is run at the behest of big business. Whether that is true or not, the way to change things is for people to take more control of the process of government — and the only legitimate way for this to happen is through parliament.

In each of these areas, a common theme recurs: the notion that knowledge is good, and can be our defence against wrong-doing.

So to all those who would wish for higher ethical standards in Irish business, I therefore suggest two words to write on their banner: on one side, *competition*; on the other, *openness*. Profits and ethics are not mutually exclusive.

6

Two Worlds, Light Years Apart

Fr Peter McVerry

During the five years of Ireland's greatest economic growth, from 1996 to 2001, five years of unparalleled prosperity, the number of homeless people in our country almost doubled. How could this be? We could analyse the effect of prosperity on the price of housing; the demand for private rented accommodation due to the inflow of people seeking work in the expanding economy; the growing number on the local authorities' housing lists due to the inability of many middle-class people to obtain a mortgage; the difficulty of attracting volunteers to work with the homeless due to the long hours of working and commuting that almost everyone is subjected to; and so on and so on. These technical problems undoubtedly determine the level of homelessness. But to understand how the numbers of homeless could almost double during five years of prosperity, we have to look deeper.

THE PARABLE

John lives in an apartment on the top floor of a house. Eight o'clock in the morning and he pulls the curtains — the sun shines in. He looks out of the window at the mountains in the distance rolling down to the sea. He sees the ships moving in and out of the harbour and the yachts on the sea. The mountains are sometimes covered in snow; at other times, it is a luscious sea of green. The sun shows the scene in all its beauty. He says: "It is a beautiful day. It is great to be alive."

Jim lives in the basement flat of the same house. Eight o'clock in the morning and he pulls the curtains —nothing happens. The sun cannot get in. He looks out the window and all he sees is the whitewashed wall of the outside toilet. He cannot see the mountains, or the sea, or the yachts, or the sun. He doesn't know what sort of day it is.

Here you have two people, looking out of the same house, at the same time of the day, into the same back garden. But they have two totally different views. There is a view from the top and a view from the bottom. Both views are equally valid — although one is admittedly more attractive than the other!

THE REALITY

John is a managing director of a large company. He has a good, pensionable salary, with regular bonuses and share options. He works very hard, often having to travel abroad to attend meetings, and frequently working at home until late in the evening. He lives in a fine house in a very fashionable neighbourhood on the southside. His children went to the same fee-paying school as he did and are planning to follow in their father's footsteps when they graduate from college. His family are, of course, enrolled in VHI. John takes his family on holiday twice a year.

If you were to ask John what he thinks of the structures of Irish society, he would be fulsome in their praise.

- The educational system has been very good to him; it gave him an excellent education, allowing him to compete with the best of his international competitors, and it is now doing the same for his children.

- The housing opportunities open to him were excellent; he has a lovely house in a lovely area and when his children are grown up and have moved out, he can sell the house and buy a nice little bungalow for himself and the wife in another nice little area.

- The job market was very supportive. He had a very good college degree and it was only a matter of choosing which of the jobs he was offered. At some point in the future, he will probably seek a new career or new challenges. With his qualifications and experience, there will be no difficulty in finding a suitably rewarding and satisfying position in another company.

- The health service is excellent; he has ready access to the family GP or to consultants, to inpatient hospital treatment or to surgery.

Jim is unemployed. He had been a manual worker on the docks, but with the growth of technology, he was no longer needed. He is too old now to retrain and there are few manual jobs left for which he could apply. He lives in a flat in a local authority complex. His flat is beautiful, but the stairwells and common balconies are covered in graffiti and smell of urine. His neighbours are alcoholics and frequently have fierce drunken rows in the middle of the night, which keep them all awake. Drug-dealing goes on all day and most of the night and he can see it all happening from his window. He is scared that his children will end up taking drugs. He would love to get out of there but he doesn't have enough points to get a house of his own. His children all left school when they were fifteen. They wanted the money they could make in the local supermarket as their father was unable to give them much from his dole money. He could not persuade them to stay on in school. They told him they would never get a decent job as long as they were living in this estate, so they may as well take now what they could get.

If you were to ask Jim what he thinks of the structures of Irish society, you would get a very different reply to that of John:

- The educational system taught him to read and write, but otherwise it was of no benefit to him. Few children in his

neighbourhood completed second-level education and nobody he knew had ever gone to college.

- The housing system is awful. He is stuck in a flat in which he
  doesn't want to live but there is a dire shortage of local authority accommodation and long waiting lists.

- The job market has collapsed. He hasn't worked for ten years
  and he has given up hoping that he will one day work again.
  His children are stuck in dead-end jobs that will not last.

- The health service is appalling; he faces long waiting times to
  see his GP, long waiting lists to see consultants or to have non-
  emergency operations.

Both John and Jim live in the same country, have gone through
the same educational system, competed in the same labour market. But they have two totally different views of Irish society;
there is a view from the top and a view from the bottom. Both
views are equally valid. But that is not, in itself, the problem.

BACK TO THE PARABLE

Now imagine that at the back of the house in which John and Jim
live is a large garden. It is completely unkempt. The grass is three
feet tall, the weeds cannot believe their luck (indeed there are
probably some new, previously unknown, species of weed growing there!), there is rubbish piled high in the corner and the rail-
ings that surround the garden are rusted and broken. Imagine
that John, who lives in the top flat, is the owner of the house. John
has some money saved from the rental income of the tenants in
the house and he is wondering what he will do with it to improve
the house. It is perfectly rational to decide that the back garden is
such an eyesore that he will have to do it up. It completely spoils
his view from the window. So he cleans up the garden, employs a
landscape gardener, replaces the fence, builds a lovely fountain in
the middle, plants beautiful flowers in colourful flowerbeds dot-
ted throughout the garden. This investment not only makes it
much more attractive to live at the top of the house, but it un-

doubtedly increases the value of the house. Everyone who visits John compliments him on what he has done.

However, the beautifully restored garden is irrelevant to Jim. He has no view of the garden; he doesn't even have a door to give him access to the garden. Jim had suggested to John that he relocate the outside toilet. That would have improved Jim's view of the garden immeasurably. But John did not think that that was a priority. It would have been expensive to do, and anyway the toilet was working perfectly well where it was. He did, it is true, paint the toilet wall. It was now a beautiful sky blue.

John didn't have to live in the basement. He had no idea of how the toilet wall was impacting on the quality of Jim's view. Of course, Jim had tried to explain it to John, but John wasn't impressed. Anyway, what did Jim expect for €120 a week — a penthouse suite?

Now, John had another thought! Now that the value of the house had increased, he was entitled to increase the rent paid by the tenants. So he announced a 25 per cent increase in rent. But Jim was unable to afford this increase. John told him he had to leave. That was just market reality. John was a businessman, not a social worker. Sentimentality reduces your bank balance like nothing else.

So to Jim in the basement, the very reasonable — reasonable to John, that is — decision that John had taken was, at best, irrelevant; at worst, it led to him becoming homeless. John could never understand those who criticised his decision to renovate the garden.

BACK TO REALITY

How could the government produce a National Health Strategy that was going to cost €12 billion over the next ten years, but which failed to increase the eligibility level for medical cards holders, if they understood how people on low incomes are afraid to go to their doctor until their health problems reach crisis point, because they cannot afford the expense? But people on low incomes live in a different world to that of the decision-makers. Two worlds, both important, side by side, but light years apart.

The problem was not that John and Jim had different views;
the problem arises because all the decisions in our society are
made by those with the view from the top — and they have no
feeling for the views of those at the bottom. They *know* the views of
those at the bottom, they have read reports, they have visited the
places they live, they have a *concept* of what their views are. But
they have no *feel* for those views. There are two different worlds,
side by side, but light years apart.

John *knows* that demolishing the toilet wall would improve
Jim's view. But the cost is too much, it is too inconvenient, there is
little point since the toilet is already working perfectly. To John,
Jim is a bit obsessive about the toilet, he is being unreasonable;
indeed he is a bit ungrateful. I mean, it's not that John doesn't *care*.
Of course he does. If he didn't, he would not have given Jim the
flat in the first place. He always makes sure that repairs are done
quickly and efficiently. Jim took the flat knowing that the toilet
was there. The view from the window is no big deal, says John,
not realising that it was the view from *his* window that prompted
him to clean up the garden!

The effects of power depend on the *relationship* between the
person who has power and the groups who are affected by the
use of that power.

Suppose that Jim was a very close friend of John's. John would
have had no hesitation in demolishing the toilet. If it was beyond
his means, he might have come to some arrangement with Jim to
increase the rent to a level Jim could afford and put the extra income into the demolition of the toilet. John's friendship with Jim
would have given him not only a *concept* of how much the toilet
means to Jim, but also a *feel* for what it means to Jim. And because
of his relationship to Jim, he would want to do something about it.

The sort of society we build depends on the decisions that
some people make. Those who make the decisions in our society
are almost always middle-class, comfortably off and well-
educated. They understand the culture from which they have
come, the view from the top. Decision makers have, inevitably, a
stronger affinity with some groups than with others, and so the

concerns of those groups will be much more easily understood and felt than the concerns of others. Good people make bad decisions not because of a defect in moral values but because of a defect in vision. Because they are unaware. They are unaware of the problems, feelings and struggles of those at the bottom of society. Hence the priority for decision-makers ought to be to reach out, to understand, to befriend, to listen to the views, feelings and concerns of those who are on the margins.

How could a Minister introduce a Bill on Intellectual Disabilities which succeeded in angering and alienating everyone with disabilities and every organisation working with them, if the Minister had a feeling for the difficulties, frustrations and feelings of those who are disabled? No doubt the Minister was thinking of the legal and financial problems which would be created for successive Governments if the Bill gave people with disabilities the rights which they demanded. Two different worlds, both important, intimately connected, but light-years apart.

To build a just society, decision-makers have to spend much more time in shelters for the homeless, refuges for battered women, the overcrowded homes of those on the local authorities' waiting lists, in the drug clinics and on the streets, with mothers of children with special needs, with those dependent on public health services, with those on low incomes unable to qualify for medical cards. Only then will they begin to see the view from the bottom, to feel the feelings of those who have that view. To build a just society, decision-makers may have to decide that they just do not have time to open new pubs or motorways.

A decision is made to cut €54 million from the overseas aid budget. This decision is made by someone sitting at a computer screen trying to balance figures in different columns. They are insulated from the consequences of their decision. Of course, they understand that "projects" will not be completed and others will not start up. But they do not hear the cries of street children orphaned by AIDS, or the mourning of mothers as they bury their children who died from lack of food or lack of medicine. Two different worlds, both important, both interlinked, but light years apart.

The core, then, to creating a more just society in which all groups can participate more equally is to ensure that the view of those from the bottom is firmly and clearly articulated, listened to and respected by those who make the decisions in our society. This rarely happens. No doubt the Minister for Finance, when preparing the budget, will carefully read the submissions from IBEC, the banks and other influential groups. But what happens to the submission from the Ballymun Unemployment Centre? "Sure what would they know about the economy and the effects of tax cuts on the rate of inflation?" But while they may not have studied economics, the perspective of the Ballymun Unemployment Centre is central to creating a more just society because they have something to offer which no third-level institute can teach: they can show us what it is like to live at the bottom of society.

The application of theoretical principles will never, on its own, produce a just society. The study of ethics may well produce a body of principles which are the result of rational thought. But the *soul* of ethics is a *sense of solidarity*. Ethical principles may be natural and reasonable — from a certain viewpoint. "Treat slaves with kindness" may have seemed a lofty ethical principle to slave-owners but I'm not sure that the slaves would have agreed! What appears to be a natural, reasonable thing to do depends on the view that you have. And it is our solidarity with others which challenges that view.

We live in a very divided society, and indeed in a society that is becoming more and more divided. All the decisions in our society are made by those who are on one side. Those on the other side are excluded and marginalised. Their view of Irish society is very different. It does not have any greater *validity* than the view from the top — but it does have *priority*, precisely because it is the view of those who have been excluded. If building a just society depends on the decisions that some people make, then reaching out across the divide to hear, respect and understand how the other side live and feel and think and value and suffer is the essential requisite to building a just society.

7

ETHICAL CHOICES WE NEED TO MAKE TO CREATE A JUST SOCIETY

John Lonergan

I have the audacity to believe that people everywhere can have three meals a day for their bodies, education and culture for their minds and dignity, equality and freedom for their spirits.
— Martin Luther King

Irish society has undergone phenomenal change over the past decade or so. Indeed, no other generation of our people have experienced such rapid and dramatic change in such a short period of time. Like every other era, our current society has its pros and cons. There is little doubt that many things in our modern society are positive, progressive and a vast improvement on the past. However, few would argue that we have the ideal society, so for this particular article I am focusing on the ethical changes we need to make to create an all-inclusive just society in the future.

Nowadays, materialism, consumerism and the monetary economy totally dominate our whole society. They have become engrained in our culture and are becoming more and more deep-rooted. In addition, there is an unbalanced emphasis on individual rights, self-interest and self-actualisation and personal materialistic success. Not surprisingly, lurking closely in the background are the dark shadows of greed, jealousy and selfishness. We have sold our souls in the pursuit of money; it is no coincidence that one of the most popular TV programmes is *Who Wants to be a Millionaire?* Money has become our new God. It is now almost impossible to distinguish us from any other Western European people. Caring and sharing, once part of our very nature, has been replaced by a new culture of *"mé féinism"*. We have convinced ourselves that we are modern, independent, educated and self-sufficient and that money will buy happiness and human fulfilment. We indoctrinate our young people in the open market philosophy of the winner takes all and, naturally, many of our people are unable to measure up or go the pace and they are instantly labelled "failures", becoming surplus to requirements.

We have double standards: on the one hand we encourage one sector of society, inevitably our more affluent, to have unlimited expectations and to place a very high premium on their contribution; while on the other hand we neglect, ignore and suppress the ambitions of other sectors, usually the poor, by paying them a pittance. Why do we support and sustain a system that pays one group in society €2,000 per day for their services while at the other end of the social ladder we expect people on Social Welfare to live on a little over €100 per week. The well-off openly confuse needs with luxuries and are unable to recognise or accept when they have enough, while those at the bottom of the social scale remain homeless, destitute, neglected and surrounded by hopelessness. We are now beginning to realise that there is a huge price to pay in human and social terms for our new "progressive" world. We are a most divided and fragmented society where the "haves" are becoming more arrogant, self-righteous and intolerant and the "have-nots" feel angry, disillusioned, exploited and humiliated. We are now seeing at first hand the fallacy of the once-popular slogan "rising tides lift all boats". Rising tides may lift all boats but the problem with our modern society is that only a very elite group own boats or are taken on board as passengers, while so many are left to "paddle their own canoe".

In our modern society, loneliness and isolation are much more prevalent; violence and aggression is an everyday experience;

drugs and alcohol are resorted to by many, mainly those who are socially excluded, to ease their pain. One sector of our society has no contact or perception of how another sector lives and they do not want to know. We have little sense of community and identity. No wonder then that we have so much social disruption, personal aggression, loneliness, disconnection, addiction and violence in our society. Is this the price we must pay for allowing consumerism and materialism to totally infiltrate and dominate our society? Have we bought a "pig in a poke" by falling for the propaganda that materialism guarantees human fulfilment and happiness?

How can we create a fair society? I feel that to do so we must examine the very structures of our current society to find the answers. Indeed, I believe that our modern society is so fundamentally flawed that it will require major restructuring if we are ever to create a genuine, fair and equal society.

We must begin by putting human needs and values at the very top of our priority list — *people first* must be our new motto. We must involve people of all ages in deciding their futures by putting in place at local and national level adequate consultative structures to ensure that people from every sector of our society have an opportunity to have their say and to be heard. In addition, we must actively promote and enshrine in our everyday lives human values based on respect, human rights, equal opportunity, compassion, justice and forgiveness. These values must become the very foundation of our future society. All policy issues and developments must be tested and measured against these principles.

There is an appalling lack of respect for the person throughout our society and as usual the biggest sufferers are our most vulnerable and broken, the old, the sick, the mentally ill, the unemployed, the poor, the homeless, the addicted, minority groups, refugees, the Travelling community, those suffering from disability, the socially disadvantaged, wrongdoers and many other groups and individuals. A society that is selective about those it respects is fundamentally flawed and bigoted and is incapable of providing real justice and equality for all of its people. We are all contributing to this destructive culture and we must start by examining our own behaviour and attitudes. We must *do* rather than say. All the various sectors, services and institutions of our society must demonstrate respect for all human beings and ensure that this is a core value. Employers must demonstrate through their dealings with their staff that they respect their workers collectively and individually. Employees must reciprocate. Our educational system must promote the principle of respect for all. Service providers must treat all those whom they serve with dignity and respect. Parents must show respect in all their dealings and interactions with their children and with others. The justice system must ensure that all people, including the wrongdoer, are treated with respect. Treating people with genuine respect irrespective of their age, sex, status, colour or background must be promoted and practised throughout our society. Ultimately progress in this area will depend on changing attitudes. We control our own attitudes, so change begins with us, you and me.

Guaranteeing basic human rights for all our people must also be high on our list of priorities. We have become very selective in our application and interpretation of what basic human rights really demand of us as a society. As already stated, we are a very divided, fragmented, unjust society. Amazingly, we have made it like this; it did not happen by accident. The result is that the circumstances of birth too often decide the direction of our lives. For some it is a life of comfort, support, opportunity and fulfilment. For others, usually those born into poverty and social disadvantage, life is really tough with few opportunities to grow and develop to their full potential. Why do we allow such discrimination to exist? Every child must have a fundamental right to a bed, food, clothes, medical care, full education, work and other basic human rights. We are a long way from achieving this objective — is it even on our agenda?

Providing equal opportunities for all our children is a long-held aspiration of Irish society. As a society we are good on aspirations and weak on delivery. The reality is that for many thousands of our children, again mostly those born into poverty and social disadvantage, equal opportunity is an unobtainable dream. In every aspect of their lives, they are at a huge disadvantage. For them, doors of opportunity are few and far between. These children quickly pick up the vibes that they are second-class citizens and their self-esteem suffers accordingly. Little wonder then that many of them drop out of formal education at a very young age. They have few work opportunities and they quickly become disillusioned and disconnected from mainstream society. They are destined to carry the "loser" label throughout their lives.

The contrast between their situation and that of their more affluent peers is immense. The challenge is: can we bridge this gap? Can we level the playing pitch so as to ensure that all our children are cherished equally? Of course we can, *but have we the will and the generosity to do it?* And equal opportunity does not end with children. Sadly, the challenge to deliver equal opportunity to all our people will, I believe, remain an aspiration for many more generations and will never be achieved if we continue to rely on our present socio-economic and political structures to deliver it.

Those of us who have become more affluent and successful have also become very hardhearted and self-righteous. We have developed a sense of superiority and indestructibility, believing that we are totally independent and self-sufficient but not realising that we are living a very privileged life often in total isolation from other less successful groups. We have little understanding of human vulnerability and many of us are incapable of empathising with the suffering of our less fortunate neighbours. Our expectation that all human beings have the ability to achieve our standards in life is unrealistic. By virtue of our humanity, we are all imperfect and there is no such species as the perfect human being. We are all flawed and blessed simultaneously but many of us are lucky that we can manage and control our weaknesses or conceal them. Unfortunately, others are not so lucky and struggle throughout their lives trying to cope with the consequences of physical, mental or emotional difficulties or abuse and burdened with the brutal consequences of poverty. We are all vulnerable and frequently need help and support. In return, we must be prepared to help those whose lives are broken and disconnected. Compassion has to be an essential component of any fair and just society.

Justice for all our people is a core principle with which we all readily agree and support in theory. But we have failed miserably to create a just society and in fact injustice is endemic throughout our society and is the root cause of many of our social problems. I am going to confine myself to highlighting three of the most important and influential factors in determining a just society. They are housing policy, health and other care services and educational opportunities.

There are major disparities and serious injustices directly linked to our current housing policy and structures. Indeed, housing is at the very hub of our divided society and once again money is the deciding factor. Those in our society who have money can buy quality housing with all the most wonderful support structures and luxuries in place. A high social status is automatically acquired as a bonus. The open and free market decides the price one pays and only the rich can really compete. But the open and free market is often manipulated and exploited. A small elite group in our society have controlled building land and managed the market for years. They are our "successes". Meanwhile thousands of young couples are mortgaged to the hilt for thirty or forty years, destined to slave for the rest of their lives just to repay their debts. Where is the justice in this?

At the opposite end of the social spectrum, many people are destined to live their lives in "ghettoes" with few support services and demoralising and dehumanising cultures and environments. Add to this the fact that homeless children sleep on the streets in cardboard boxes. Also, is it just a coincidence that over 75 per cent of all Dublin-born prisoners come from small pockets in six separate postal districts of Dublin city? Or why does the address on job application forms either greatly improve or seriously impede an applicant's prospects? Is this not a disgrace? Our housing policy and strategies have played a crucial role in developing our socially divided society. We must tackle this issue immediately if we are remotely serious about developing a just society.

Our educational system has also failed many thousands of our children, mostly but not exclusively those at the bottom of our social status ladder. We hate to hear this, but our formal educational system is very much a two-tier system and (fees or no fees) money still plays a significant role in the quality of education available to our children. In our most disadvantaged areas, second-level education is still out of the reach of many children. Indeed, many do not even complete primary level. In addition, a recent survey covering access to third-level education highlighted appalling discrepancies between affluent and disadvantaged areas in Dublin. In many instances, the discrepancy was as high as seventy per cent. Social circumstances rather than academic ability is too often the deciding factor. It is not that everyone must go to third level; it is about choice.

Education is not the be all and end all in terms of justice but it is one of the most significant factors. Children who miss out on formal education are at a huge disadvantage in modern Ireland and one of the most serious repercussions is that it greatly reduces their job prospects. As a society we have an obligation to ensure that every child has free and equal access to all levels of education. In particular we must ensure that money is not the deciding factor.

The provision of comprehensive and quality health and other care services for all must be a fundamental facet of our future society. Presently access to many such services is over-dependent on financial resources. For example, hospital waiting lists can disappear overnight provided one could pay. I had a personal experience some time ago when I required an X-ray on my neck and shoulder. When I rang for the appointment I was asked whether I was "private" or "public". When I naïvely responded that it did not matter, I was quickly told that it did, there was a waiting period of three weeks if I went public whereas if I availed of private treatment I could have it done that afternoon. I paid and jumped the queue. We must eliminate such unfair advantages for one sector of society over another. Money must not be the deciding factor because when it is the poor and the most vulnerable will once again be the main sufferers.

A just society must also take good care of its senior citizens. Many of our elderly live their lives in loneliness and isolation. We must develop the infrastructure and support services to ensure that they can live out their lives as full and equal members of our society. Above all they must not be treated as "disposables". The mentally ill are another group often neglected in our modern society. Many live in appalling conditions and as a society we should be ashamed of the way we treat these most vulnerable people. Caring for the sick, the elderly and the disabled in our society must be one of our top priorities and indeed our status as a just and caring society must be measured against how well we meet this responsibility.

A further basic requirement of a just society is to promote and practice a genuine and generous commitment to forgiveness. In today's society, we are all finding it more and more difficult to forgive one another. Not only are we unable to forgive but we appear to gloat and get enjoyment out of the misfortune of others. Self-righteousness and condemnation are now rampant throughout our society and those who do wrong are ostracised within our society and are quickly awarded the "disgraced" tag. This is a most hurtful and damaging label to inflict on any person. Who gave us the right to be so arrogant and superior to our fellow man? As human beings we are all sinners and we are in no position to point the finger at others — we all have a dark side. To forgive those who have hurt us by word or deed is always very difficult but the reality is that we all do wrong and we all need to be forgiven at some stage in our lives. If we cannot forgive those who have offended us, we cannot expect to be forgiven ourselves when we do wrong. To be forgiven is often the ultimate therapy for those who have done wrong and who are genuinely sorry. How we respond to this challenge will decide how mature, civilised and tolerant our society will be in the future.

Finally, I must mention the media, who are now the most dominant influence within our society. They have played a central role in shaping our modern society and will continue to do so in the future. Of course, the media has been responsible for opening up our society and making it more transparent. They have also forced many individuals, State institutions and powerful groups to answer for their abuse of power. The media must continue to inform Irish society and to be courageous in investigating and reporting on corruption and wrongdoing. However, there is a real danger that an all-powerful media may become arrogant and not adhere to the principles of fairness, honesty, integrity and justice and this in turn may lead to an abuse of power by them. We need a responsible and diligent media but not at any cost. They must ensure that those under scrutiny and investigation are given every opportunity of reply, that innocent people are not damaged or demonised and that there is always balance and objectivity underpinning their work. They must also resist and remain aloof from the influence of the heavily financed "spin doctoring" industry. But most importantly of all, the media must ensure that they do not become defensive when they themselves are being criticised, that they do not attempt to suppress such criticism and that they acknowledge that the common good is best served if the public are the final arbiters.

The values highlighted in this article are some of the most essential elements in underpinning a just society — one which respects and nurtures all its children equally; insists that people and their human needs are sacrosanct; ensures that its wealth and resources are distributed fairly and equally and guarantees basic human rights for all its people. Perhaps a dream, but, as Abraham Lincoln said "the probability that we may fail in the struggle ought not to deter us from the support of a cause we believe to be just".

8

ECOLOGY AND ETHICS

Sean McDonagh SSC

Our modern world has thrown up major new challenges to ethical thinking and practice. At the moment a host of serious environmental problems are facing people here in Ireland and globally. In this chapter I will look at two issues, namely genetic engineering and climate change.

I believe our present moral framework is ill-equipped to deal competently with the ethics of either genetic engineering or climate change. Genetic engineering is a new and powerful technology that can literally transform not just human life but life itself. I will argue that an exclusively human-centred or homocentric ethical focus is not capable of dealing adequately with something as complex as genetic engineering. Therefore I believe that we must broaden the ethical focus to include other creatures and the planet itself. Furthermore, in the traditional manuals of ethics, the focus of ethical concern was normally on the impact of human behaviour on people today. Both genetic engineering and global warming invite us to take a longer view, namely the impact of our current behaviour on future generations and on the planet.

WESTERN ETHICAL TRADITION WAS HUMAN-CENTRED

Aristotle, whose impact on Western thought is enormous, held that since "nature makes nothing without some end in view, nothing to no purpose, it must be that nature has made (animals and plants) for the sake of man".[5] This idea that animals and plants are created for humankind — either by God or the processes of nature — has dominated Western attitudes to animals, plants and the rest of creation for many centuries.

From this viewpoint, since animals and plants exist for human beings, our behaviour towards them is not governed by moral considerations. It is only in the past decade that the cruelty involved in factory farming or blood sports has been discussed from an ethical perspective. Even then, the proscription on cruelty towards animals arises, not so much from inherent rights that animals might have, but from the understanding that any form of cruelty is unbecoming and, therefore, unethical for rational beings.

THE CHRISTIAN TRADITION SUPPORTED HUMAN-CENTRED ETHICS

It is also true that certain elements within the Judeo-Christian tradition have strongly reinforced the Aristotelian legacy. This is particularly the case when one considers the traditional interpretation given to Gen 1:26–28. "Increase and multiply and dominate the earth". The text is often interpreted, mistakenly, according to contemporary scripture scholars, as giving humans a licence to dominate the earth and do whatever they wish with animals and plants. Elsewhere in the biblical tradition there were very few, if any, moral precepts to guide and structure the interaction between humans and the rest of creation. Humans could change and transform the natural world in the most extensive way without feeling that they had transgressed any moral precept.

The historian, Keith Thomas, points out that at the beginning of the sixteenth century, just as modern science was finding its

---

[5] Aristotle (1985), *Politics*, Penguin, London.

feet, neither Western literature nor theological tradition ascribed any intrinsic meaning to the natural world or accorded it any rights apart from its role in serving humankind.[6] From the theological perspective it was argued that humans had intrinsic value because they were made in the "image and likeness of God" (Gen 1:26). Their role was to be "masters of the fish of the sea, the birds of heaven and all living animals on the earth" (Gen 1:28). No other creature bore this *Imago Dei* (image of God) stamp. Animals and plants were viewed as lacking rational faculties, self-consciousness and often even sentience and hence had no intrinsic worth in themselves. They only had instrumental value. Their role was to serve the needs of humankind for the necessities of life and they could also be used for entertainment.

FRANCISCAN TRADITION

It is true that within the Judeo-Christian tradition there is a strand that sees humans as stewards of creation (Gen 2:15). Unfortunately, as Clive Ponting points out in his *Green History of the World*, "although the idea that humans have a responsibility to preserve the natural world of which they are merely guardians can be traced through a succession of thinkers it has remained a minority tradition".[7] Unfortunately, St Francis's kinship with brother Sun, Sister Moon and all creation was very much a minority position. His fraternal attitude did not inform the Western approach to nature. In fact, it did not even survive in any effective way within the congregation which he founded.

ANTHROPOCENTRISM IS DEEP-ROOTED AND PERVASIVE IN WESTERN CULTURE

The seemingly almost unbridgeable chasm between humans and the rest of creation was further widened by the rise of modern science and technology in Europe. Since the sixteenth century the

---

[6] Keith Thomas (1983), *Man and the Natural World*, Pantheon Books, New York, p. 35.

[7] Clive Ponting (1991), *A Green History of the World*, Sinclair Stevenson, p. 142.

writings of scientists like Francis Bacon, Rene Descartes and Isaac Newton, and philosophers like Hobbes, Locke and Jeremy Bentham have further fuelled this human-centred focus. In the succeeding centuries, science, and its handmaiden technology, was viewed as a tool in the hands of human beings giving them power to dominate and manipulate the earth in whatever way they saw fit in order to secure human well-being and betterment.

EXTENSIVE ENVIRONMENTAL DAMAGE

While individuals like the poet Gerard Manly Hopkins were aware of the darker side of technology in the late nineteenth century, it was only after the Second World War that a more general discussion began to take place about what humans were doing to the environment. Some authors date the rise of modern environmental consciousness among non-specialists to the publication of *Silent Spring* in 1962. In the book, Rachel Carson gave graphic detail of the impact that organochlorines like DDT where having on bird life in the United States. Since then, we have become more aware of the fact that human technologies have inflicted huge damage on other creatures and on planet earth itself. The damage is not restricted to a single river bank for which Hopkins wept in *Binsey Poplars*. Every ecosystem on the planet has been affected. The damage is enormous and, in some situations like the extinction of species, it is irreversible. This has implications for every species alive today and especially for future generations.

THE STORY OF THE UNIVERSE

Any adequate ethical framework for dealing with these moral predicaments must be based on our contemporary understanding of the relationship between humans and the rest of the natural world. Current studies in genetics and evolutionary biology tell us that humans are not separate from the rest of nature. We now know that all life on earth came from a common ancestry. Despite the fact that the living world branched off into various paths and seems very different in size when we compare an insect with an elephant, we all have quite similar cell structures. Humans are close cousins of the chimpanzee. We share 95 per cent of our DNA with them. What unites us is much more significant than the mere five per cent that divides us. Chimpanzees and humans have common anatomical features so the similarities may not surprise us. But even when we look at much smaller and seemingly different creatures like beetles, over 50 per cent of the DNA is common to both species.

When scientists study mammals or insects in any detail, they find that they are extraordinarily complex and wonderful beings. The more we learn about other species, the more we realise that they cannot be mere objects for our consumption or pleasure. More and more, we are beginning to see them as subjects and as such they ought to evoke from us an attitude of wonder and respect. This, of course, will mean that our engagement with them carries a deep ethical dimension.

From a theological perspective, Christians can say that God created all the creatures of the web of life with the same love and care that He/She lavished on human beings. The more we learn about the story of the universe and, especially about the story of life on earth, the more fascinating and mind-boggling that story becomes. It certainly invites us humans to have a deep respect for all the community of living beings — people, animals and plants. None of these will thrive if the earth, the waters of the world and the air are poisoned. We cannot have healthy beetles, chimps or humans on a sick planet.

We need this holistic approach to many questions today, including ethics. Since anthropocentric ethical norms did not sensitise us to the damage that was taking place or guide our behaviour towards a less destructive way of interacting with the rest of creation, we now need a more eco-centred and theocentric moral framework if we are to successfully address these vital contemporary moral issues.

ETHICS MUST FOCUS ON THE COMMUNITY OF LIFE

Fr Thomas Berry, an American priest who has written extensively
on environmental issues for decades, feels that contemporary ethics must focus its concerns on the larger community of the living.
He states that

> the human community is subordinate to the ecological
> community. The ecological imperative is not derivative
> from human ethics. Human ethics is derived from the eco-
> logical imperative which is the well-being of the compre-
> hensive community, not the well-being of the human
> community. The earth is a single ethical system, as the uni-
> verse is a single ethical system.[8]

This is the first principle of an ecological ethic. Such an ethic
would demand a legal framework where the rights of the geological and biological as well as the human components of the earth
community are protected.

I am not arguing for what might be called a democracy of
moral behaviour — in other words, that there should be no difference between the way I treat fellow human beings and other creatures. I have no doubt about the fact that my moral responsibilities
towards other human beings will normally take precedence over
my responsibilities towards other creatures. The crucial point
about an eco-centred ethical perspective is that my engagement
with other creatures and the planet itself must now be based on
moral precepts that promote human *and* planetary well-being.

GENETIC ENGINEERING

Genetic engineering provides a good contemporary example of
the contrast between an eco-centred ethical framework and a
purely anthropocentric one. A report published in 1997 that was
commissioned by the Marine Institute of Ireland, discussed *The
Nature and Current Status of Transgenetic Atlantic Salmon*. The

---

[8] Berry, Thomas (1994), *Ethics and Ecology*, unpublished paper.

document stated that, as a result of introducing growth hormone genes into a wild North Atlantic salmon, the transgenetic fish grows rapidly and reaches enormous size. Studies have shown that within a period of fourteen months, the transgenetic salmon can weigh 37 times more than the ordinary salmon. These increases will probably secure large profits for the company producing and marketing the transgenetic salmon. The cost of the experiment to the salmon is horrendous. In technical and unemotive language, the report notes that the experiment produced "profound morphological abnormalities" in the progeny of the transgenetic salmon. These include a "disproportionate growth of the head and operculum cartilage, disimproving appearances leading ultimately to respiratory problems". The report never raised the fundamental moral question: Do human beings have a right to interfere in such a profound way with the genetic integrity of other creatures?[9]

Viewed through the prism of an anthropocentric perspective, the answer to the above question is probably yes. It would confer no rights on either the individual salmon or even on the species. It also would be neutral about the desire to make a hefty profit unless it was based on fraud or the abuse of peoples' rights. Even though the Catholic Church has attempted to develop a creation theology in recent years and in some pronouncements has begun to accept that other species have intrinsic value, many church people still work out of an anthropocentric perspective. Speaking at a conference on biotechnology in October 2002, Bishop Elio Sgreccia, vice president of the Pontifical Academy for Life, said, "There are no impediments to animal and vegetable biotechnologies." The latter "can be justified with the motive that they are for the good of man. God has conceived animals and vegetables as good creatures for man's needs," the bishop added. He did add an unspecified caution when he stated that God has also given "man the task and responsibility to govern creation", which implies a grave responsi-

---

[9] T.F. Cross and P.T. Gavlin (1996), *The Nature and Current Status of Transgenetic Salmon*, Marine Institute of Ireland, Dublin, page 6.

bility. Bishop Sgreccia emphasised that, therefore, "the use of plants and animals is legitimate, but it does not represent an absolute right. The Church has an open but conditioned position," he added. "For this reason, we ask for sales to be accompanied by a label [mentioning GMOs] and their total availability for developing countries, in keeping with criteria of solidarity and justice."[10]

The bishop focused completely on the impact of this new technology on humankind, even when he champions labelling and equity for hungry people in the Third World. The rights of other species not to be subjected to cruel experimentation or to have their genetic integrity, particularly at the species level, respected by human beings is not even raised.

Ethical principles, drawn from the wider biocentric and theological framework outlined by Berry would look on the above case in a very different way. Such an approach would insist that the genetic integrity of non-human species, especially animals, must be respected. Viewed in this way, species boundaries must be given ethical weight. This approach would find the operation involved in creating the transgenetic salmon morally repugnant, particularly since it did such damage to the anatomy of the fish. It would also point to the immense genetic damage that could be visited on the north Atlantic salmon if such transgenetic salmon escaped and mated with the wild salmon. The report outlined all the steps that were taken to prevent this happening. But Murphy's Law tells us that what can happen will happen, especially if large numbers of these transgenetic salmon are created.

Deep ecologists like Arne Naess would probably go much further and abhor all such experiments. Deep ecologists value non-human life independently of its usefulness to humankind and challenges humans to be much more respectful of other creatures.

---

[10] Zenit.org, Rome, 9 October 2002.

GLOBAL WARMING AND CLIMATE CHANGE

Another pressing contemporary ecological problem with potentially disastrous consequences is global warming. The atmospheric concentration of carbon dioxide, methane, chlorofluorocarbons (CFCs) and other "greenhouse" gases are expected to increase by 30 per cent during the next fifty years. This build-up is likely to increase the earth's surface temperature by between 1.5° and 4.5° centigrade by the year 2030. A study by a group of scientists in preparation for the international meeting on global warming in the Hague in November 2000 suggests that the "upper range of warming over the next 100 years could be far higher than was estimated in 1995".[11]

Global warming will cause major, and in the main, deleterious climatic changes. In northern latitudes, winters will probably be shorter and wetter. Sub-tropical areas might become drier and more arid and tropical ones wetter. The changes will have major, but as yet unpredictable, effects on agriculture and natural ecosystems.

Melting Ice

As the oceans warm up and expand, sea levels will rise, leading to severe flooding over lowland areas. In March 2002, scientists in the Antarctica revealed that the Larsen B ice shelf disappeared from the map, setting 500 million billion tonnes of water afloat. Glaciologists were taken aback by the speed with which the area disintegrated. It took only 31 days. This disintegration has dumped more ice into the Southern ocean than all the icebergs for the past fifty years. The reason why the ice-fields in the Antarctic are breaking up so rapidly is that the temperature in the area has increased by 2.5° centigrade in the past fifty years.

Unfortunately, the poorest countries, many of which emitted very little greenhouse gases during the last century, will suffer

---

[11] John Vidal, "Global warming is greater than predicted — study", *The Irish Times*, October 2001.

most from climate change. Much of Bangladesh and the low-lying areas of countries like Egypt will simply disappear and thus create enormous migration problems. Even first-world cities like Venice are feeling the effects of global warming as the sea rises around it. Here in Ireland, the rise in sea-levels will lead to greater coastal erosion.

Melting glaciers are also creating potential disasters. In the next five years, as many as forty lakes that have been formed by melting ice high up in the Himalayas, especially in Nepal and Bhutan, could burst their banks and cause devastation in the lowland valleys. According to Paul Brown of *The Guardian*, "there are thought to be hundreds more such liquid time bombs in India, Pakistan, Afghanistan, Tibet and China".[12] The situation is rendered more dangerous by the fact that many of these lakes are in geologically active areas. A sizeable earthquake could trigger a disaster.

More frequent and violent storms

Storms of great ferocity — like hurricane Mitch which slammed into Central America in October 1998, the devastating floods and mudslides which killed over 10,000 people on the Caribbean coast of Venezuela, and the wind storms that battered France after Christmas 1999 — will probably become more frequent. *The Guardian* (31 October 2000) surveyed the damage caused by gales and flooding in southern England at the end of October 2000 and proclaimed in banner headlines that "Global Warming: it's with us now". Unless we stabilise greenhouse gas emissions floods of similar magnitude will become a routine feature of our weather.

A joint report sponsored by the British government and climate change scientists was released at the end of April 2002. It stated that the world was warmer in the first three months of the year than at any time in the past one thousand years. The report predicts that the weather in Britain and Ireland will become

---

[12] Paul Brown, "Global warming melts glaciers and produces many unstable lakes", *The Guardian*, 17 April 2002.

warmer and more unstable. The Irish Committee on Climate Change of the Royal Irish Academy expects that temperatures in Ireland will increase by 0.25 degrees Celsius during this century.

Areas that expected to be flooded every fifty years can now expect that by 2080 they will be flooded for nine years out of ten. Storms and heavy seas will batter coastal areas during winter. The summers in Ireland and Britain will be longer and drier. Reductions in precipitation during summer may be as high as 30 per cent less than today, which will put major pressure on our water sources. The top temperatures in the south of England could reach 40° Celsius.[13] Such a major climate change will have a huge impact on agriculture and the Irish landscape.[14] If drought is a feature of summer weather, farmers may have to consider investing in irrigation technology.

Most scientists would agree with the above prediction that Irish summers will be warmer as a result of global warming. This might seem a blessing for those who have had to endure a summer like 2002. Other analysts believe that the future in Ireland may not be so rosy. They base their predictions on the fact that the melting of the Arctic ice cap may interfere with or suspend the Gulf Stream which keeps Europe warm. This would leave Ireland, and much of Northern Europe, much colder than it is now. Not a welcome scenario!

Kyoto and Ireland

At the UN-sponsored conference on climate change in Kyoto in 1997, scores of scientists from the International Panel on Climate Change (IPCC) called for a 60 per cent reduction in the use of fossil fuel. Unfortunately, the politicians attending the meeting, representing 160 countries, could only agree to a miserly 5.2 per cent

---

[13] Paul Brown, "The World's weather hotter than ever", *The Guardian*, 26 April 2002.

[14] Ann Cahill, "Days of drought and deluge loom", *The Irish Examiner*, 1 May 2002, p. 5.

reduction below the 1990 levels by the year 2010. At Kyoto, Ireland was one of the few wealthy nations that received permission to increase its "greenhouse" gas emissions. We claimed that, since we had not been industrialised in the nineteenth century, we should be allowed more leeway than other industrial countries. We were allowed to increase our greenhouse gas emissions by 13 per cent above the 1990 levels by the year 2001.

The gallop of the Celtic tiger during the mid-1990s meant that by 1998 we had already exceeded these greenhouse gas emission levels. In August 2000 the Environmental Protection Agency published a report entitled *Emissions of Atmospheric Pollutants in Ireland 1990–1998*. It stated that we had already exceeded our 2010 target by 1998 since greenhouse gas emissions had grown by 18 per cent in eight years. The annual rate of greenhouse gas emission was then over four per cent.

In response, the Department of the Environment published the *National Climate Change Strategy* to curb greenhouse gas emissions. Among the initiatives mentioned were an unspecified tax on fossil fuel, the closure or conversion of the Moneypoint coal-fired power station and reductions in the number of animals in the national herd. The document lamely admits that "transport is generally proving to be the most difficult sector in which to achieve controls on greenhouse gas emissions in most countries due to the rising vehicle numbers and increasing travel". Chapter 5 of the report deals with transport. It is vague and aspirational. The development of rail transport is mentioned on a few occasions but, for the authors of this Report, transport means road transport. After the report was published, I attempted to find out whether any government department or agency had calculated what the extra load of greenhouse gases released from the road-building programme would be. Presumably the need for these motorways springs from research on the increased volume of vehicles on the roads; therefore it ought to be quite easy to quantify what the increase in greenhouse gases will be. I called the National Roads Authority and spoke to a very helpful person who informed me that the NRA have not quantified what the increase greenhouse gas load will be. Their Environmental Impact Studies (EIS) do look at local levels of air pollution which will follow in the wake of the motorway-building programme, but they have no figures on the increase in greenhouse gas emissions.

In July 2002, the government produced another document which was subsequently presented at the World Summit on Sustainable Development in Johannesburg (26 August to 4 September 2002). The report, entitled *Making Ireland Sustainable*, acknowledges that according to the Environmental Protection Agency Ireland's emissions of greenhouse gases in the year 2000 was already 23.7 per cent above 1990 levels and under a "business-as-usual" scenario, they would increase to 37 per cent by 2010. Once again, this document is heavy on spin and what must be done. Rather feebly, it informs the readers that "it has always been recognised that, with no action, Ireland would rapidly and substantially exceed its (Kyoto) Protocol targets". It goes on to state that "significant action" is required over this decade to limit the rise in emissions to 13 per cent.[15]

In response to this report, I again called the NRA on 26 July 2002 and asked whether anyone had researched the extra greenhouse gas load that would arise from the projected increase in traffic on the proposed motorways. I spoke to an official involved with environmental policy in the NRA. While he was very helpful he confirmed that, to date, no data was available. It seems amazing that neither the NRA nor the Department of the Environment have collected such crucial data. Furthermore, neither seem to work out of any ethical framework that prioritises strategies to stabilise global climates. Hopefully these concerns will be incorporated into the National Spatial Plan, though the track record of the government in incorporating concerns about global warming into its policies and strategies to date is very poor.

From what I have written, it is clear that global warming is a very serious environmental and ethical issue. Even if all the scien-

---

[15] "Meeting Kyoto commitment seen as a 'core' challenge", *The Irish Times*, 26 July 2002, p. 5.

tific data is not at hand, given the seriousness of the issue, the precautionary principle would direct us to take what the majority of
scientists are saying very seriously. The articulation of the precautionary principle which I favour comes from a meeting of a group
of activists, scholars, scientists and lawyers which took place at
Wingspread, home of the Johnson Foundation in Racine, Wiscon-
sin, in January 1998. The group was convened by the Science and
Environmental Health Network (SEHN) to discuss the precautionary principle. The Wingspread definition of precaution contained three important elements: namely, the threat of harm; scientific uncertainty; and preventative, precautionary action. The
Wingspread statement on the precautionary principle read as follows:

> . . . when an activity raises threats of harm to human health
> or the environment, precautionary measures should be
> taken even if some cause and effect relationships are not
> fully established scientifically. In this context the proponent
> of an activity rather than the opponents should bear the
> burden of proof. The process of applying the precautionary
> principle must be open, informed and democratic and must
> include potentially affected parties. It must also involve an
> examination of the full range of alternatives, including no
> action at all.

Climate change is not just the result of a single, destructive act.
Rather, it points to the fact that the affluence enjoyed by 20 per
cent of the world's population mainly living in the northern hemisphere is having a deleterious impact on the whole planetary system, which will effect everyone, especially poor, Third World
people. The fossil fuel industry has been allowed to bring its
products to the market at relatively low cost because it has exter-
nalised the true cost of using fossil fuel onto the environment. A
significant carbon tax would reduce carbon emissions, improve
engine technology, challenge energy-wasteful lifestyles and make
available significant resources to help the Third World cope with
the problems of climate change.

LEAD FROM THE CHURCHES

I became involved in environmental issues when I worked as a missionary on the island of Mindanao in the Philippines. I experienced the destruction of the tropical forest and the impact on the tribal people, called the T'boli people, among whom I lived. As a missionary, I also became aware of the adverse effects of global warming, especially on poor people. I began to see why it must be addressed at an ethical level as well as at a technical level. Unless we address it with concrete strategies, future generations will pay the price for the selfishness of this generation. Millions of people will be condemned to live in a much less hospitable and fruitful world.

The World Council of Churches has also responded to the global warming crisis by publishing a very thorough analysis of the ecological, economic, ethical, theological and pastoral aspects of global warming in a document called *Accelerated Climate Change: Sign of Peril, Test of Faith*.[16] Looked at from a historical perspective, it is also important to remember that northern nations have consumed the lion's share of the earth's resources and have been the worst polluters. The industrial revolution began in Europe over 200 years ago. In *Signs of Peril, Test of Faith*, the authors include a graphic illustrating that between 1800 and 1988, northern countries emitted 83.7 per cent of greenhouse gases while the south, with a much larger population, only contributed 16.3 per cent. In this context, an excellent case can be made for compensating poorer countries for not polluting the global commons during the past century based on the ethical principle that "the polluter must pay". There is a growing consensus that those who cause environmental degradation should be forced, by national and international law, to compensate the victims of pollution and bear the clean-up costs.

---

[16] *Signs of Peril, Test of Faith: Accelerated Climate Change*, May 1994, World Council of Churches, 150 route de Ferney, PO Box 2100, 1221 Geneva 2, Switzerland.

THE RIGHTS OF FUTURE GENERATIONS

Global warming throws up the issue of intergenerational justice. Traditional anthropocentric ethical concerns normally deal with the impact of behaviour on individuals or communities in the here and now or, at the most, the short-term future. That is no longer an adequate framework because this generation is bringing about such massive changes to the fabric of the earth. The moral question is simple: Does this generation have the right to use up all the fossil fuel in the world, erode its topsoil, deplete the ozone layer, build up nuclear waste and destroy tropical forests in order to enable a fifth of the world's population to live in affluence? The basic principle of intergenerational justice states that future generations have the right to inherit the world in as fertile and beautiful condition as the world this generation inhabits. It applies especially in areas like global warming, protecting biodiversity and the natural systems of the planet, like the ozone layer and the waters of the world. All of these are under attack from human activity.

In this chapter, I argued that traditional ethical norms or systems were incapable of helping humankind to confront the current massive ecological challenges. The examples I have chosen — genetic engineering and global warming — cannot be adequately understood or addressed without broadening the parameters of our ethical understanding. Unfortunately, there is very little effort in Ireland, either in the Churches or among the government agencies that are dealing with these challenges, like the Department of Transport or the Department of the Environment, to address them from an ethical perspective. Unless we begin a thorough debate about these issues, we will stumble into decisions, like building massive highways or incinerators, that will have a long-term impact on lives of people and the environment. The stakes are very high. They involve the future beauty and fruitfulness of planet Earth and the well-being of all the creatures which inhabit it, especially here in Ireland.

9

CREATION AS REVELATION: A NEW ETHIC TOWARDS THE LIVING WORLD

John Feehan

A traditional interpretation of the Book of Genesis sees the earth as put there for man's benefit, to subdue and conquer and make use of, including plants and animals over which man was to have dominion, "over the fish of the sea, and over the fowl of the air, and over every living thing that moveth upon the earth". There was nothing wrong with exploiting the resources of earth to the full; these things were put there for our use. In recent decades, a new perspective has begun to emerge, influenced from two directions: the much deeper understanding of creation emanating from science on the one hand, and our growing awareness of the danger to earth's life support systems caused by our profligate and unthinking abuse of earth resources on the other. The ethical imperative is most apparent in relation to the latter, because this disruption of life support systems and the balance of nature will hurt the lives and interests of others; it will also hurt *ourselves*, which is more to the point when it comes to taking action to avert the negative outcomes predicted. In the social and political sphere, the good of others at our personal expense is not something that galvanises us into effective action as a rule, however admirable the objectives. There is a clear ethical dimension to environmental issues such as global warming, to thinning of the earth's protective ozone layer, to pollution. It is wrong for me to allow industrial effluent or silage run-off to flow into a stream; even if it does no apparent or immediate damage, I know that the interests and welfare of my neighbours downstream are affected. It is wrong for me to burn plastic waste because it poisons the air. It is wrong for me to continue to contribute in a profligate manner to the volume of greenhouse gases in the air because the global warming they cause will affect climate patterns in ways that will profoundly damage the well-being of others, not only my neighbours downstream, but my neighbour even at the other end of the earth, and my neighbour's children and grandchildren, because the effects of these actions in which I partake will unfold over generations, and may be irreversible.

Such action differs from more familiar unethical behaviour in that its effects are not immediately apparent, and indeed may never be apparent to us: it is action at a distance in time as well as in space. However carefully we look, we may discover no damage. We need to be informed by science as to what the consequences of our actions are. This is the first of many areas in which science contributes to ethical debate in environmental issues, and it is important to notice that, as is always the case, science here in no way attempts to tell us what to do; its role is to inform us of the consequences of our actions. Because we know that without the help of science we would be unaware of the consequences of our actions, there is an obligation on us to be scientifically literate enough to understand the issues involved. We cannot behave responsibly as individuals or as a society in the modern age without science.

As we have noted, the understanding which science provides does not simply tell us what to do. This may be for one of two very different reasons. Scientific understanding of particular matters may as yet be at an insufficiently detailed or advanced state to dictate a course of action that will reliably lead to a particular desired outcome; in that case, what is needed is more scientific research. This relates to matters of *how* and *why*. The other reason may be that the question now to hand is not a scientific question. It relates to *whether* a particular course of action should be followed, action made newly possible in many cases by scientific and technological advance: presenting us with ethical dilemmas which are more familiar today in relation to genetic and medical matters but which have environmental contexts as well, in relation to genetic engineering for example.

One of the greatest environmental crises confronting us today is the loss of biodiversity. We live at a time when the colour is draining from the rainbow of life's extravagant diversity like sand from an hour glass. The colours of life's rainbow have of course slowly changed through geological time, and each colour has over time constantly altered its hue as evolution has played symphonies with its possibilities. But what is happening today is different. The rate at which species are becoming extinct because of us is between 1,000 and 10,000 times what it would be without us. Edward Wilson (1992) estimated that at the present time we are exterminating 27,000 species a year, but the actual figure may well be much greater than this. The great majority we do not even know the names of, even if we accept the conservative estimate that of the tens of millions of species of plants, animals, fungi, protists and microbes alive on earth today only about ten per cent even have names. In Wilson's estimate a further twenty per cent would become extinct at present rates within thirty years. Terry Erwin believes that at present rates of extinction half of all species will disappear during this century.[17] There is considerable professional disagreement among professional biologists about the precise extent of the reduction in biodiversity, but to become distracted or preoccupied with whether this or that is the correct figure is to fiddle while Rome burns. There can be do doubt that what is happening is catastrophic.

More immediately, the reduction in biodiversity affects the well-being of ourselves and others in a variety of ways. Again, more to the point insofar as action is concerned, it affects my future well-being, especially in the way the loss may include species

---

[17] Irwin, T.L. (1996), "Biodiversity at Its Utmost: Tropical Forest Beetles" in M.J. Reaka-Kudla, D.E. Wilson and W.O. Wilson (eds.), *Biodiversity II: Understanding and Protecting Our Biological Resources*, 27–40. Washington DC, Joseph Henry Press.

which could prove of enormous future benefit by providing new drugs, or genetic resources which the more advanced science of the future may be able to turn to our human benefit in all sorts of ways which are not now apparent. But there is a much deeper ethical dimension to the loss of biodiversity, which comes into focus especially in the light of the vastly enriched understanding of the nature of life that recent advances in biology and genetics present us with, allied with the recent revolutionary development in our understanding of cosmic and organic evolution.

A special, indeed unique, role for the human species is central to the Christian view of creation. At an earlier time, that centrality extended even to man's home, the earth itself, seen as the centre of the universe — not that there was any real *evidence* for this, but it seemed appropriate in the context of the prevailing worldview that it should be so. The scientific discoveries of Copernicus, Kepler and Galileo showed that this position was untenable, and it was in due course abandoned. In much the same way, organic evolution has forced the abandonment of the notion that mankind (*sic*) is the pinnacle of material creation, other creatures arranged in a chain of being beneath him and all the choirs of angels, immaterial beings entirely, above. But the evolution paradigm has been slowly, painfully, incrementally absorbed into the Christian view of creation, each increment hedged about with conditions that attempt to protect the integrity of the Christian message, so that mankind, and each individual person, could continue to remain unique, the only creature with an immortal soul destined for everlasting bliss. This partial acceptance of the evolutionary perspective has its eyes fixed on keeping the essentials of the received worldview intact; evolutionary tenets are tacked on in a way which does not upset the existing balance, with the result that the blinding light which an open-minded, open-spirited acceptance of what science reveals to us about the nature of life offers us is not allowed to shine upon creation and our role in it — and the powerful ethical imperative this sets up is not perceived.

What this unfolding of science demonstrates is that we are all truly related, brother and sister, not in the metaphorical sense we might once have thought, but in truth. All living things have developed from a common ancestry by the complex concatenation of processes we call evolution. There is a tree of life with repeatedly dichotomous branches. On the "twigs" nearest to us are the other creatures to which we are most closely related — in our case the "anthropoid" apes and more distantly other primates — but ultimately, you and I are brother and sister, in rough order of decreasing affinity, with other vertebrates, insects and worms and snails, with plants and fungi, protists and microbes. Science, in its modern sophistication, is even able to give us the degree of genetic affinity with increasing precision. We are all governed by the same evolutionary processes. We all have the same fundamental make-up: not simply in the sense that our bodies are all made up of cells, but that these cells have essentially the same machinery: the same biochemical pathways, the same mechanism of inheritance, the same complex suites of enzymes and other proteins, on levels of utterly extraordinary complexity which the non-biologist has little awareness of. The complexity of other creatures on this level is of the same order as our own: in no sense is it less.

Those who profess faith in God must ponder the implications of all this for religious faith. But whether they are comfortable with this way of thinking about revelation or not, there can be no doubt that God had been speaking of himself, expressing himself, revealing himself for countless epochs before human words picked up the refrain. Maybe we can see the kernel of this view of creation in the preoccupation of early Islamic and Christian philosophy with Creation as word. Even if we have some difficulty with the notion of kinship, the idea that all creatures are brother and sister, there is no questioning the fact that we are all made with the same exquisite care, that we all share the same extraordinarily complex chemistry, the scorpion and the daisy and the worm no less than our human selves. The most marvellous achievement of modern genetics has been to show in ever-greater detail the nature and extent of that relationship. I have the same kind of genetic make-up, often the very same genes, as the scorpion and the daisy and the worm, and the diversity and beauty are almost beyond belief, almost be-

yond comprehension. One corollary is that our human uniqueness
in the sight of God cannot be established on the basis of physical
complexity or the possession of some particular physical attribute.
The new biology demonstrates the true complexity of all other life
forms, every one of which (in God-talk) is made with the same loving care as we are. There is a real danger that those who are not
adequately versed in biology may fail to see the implications of
this revelation for how we are to understand the place of the human species in the universe: that it may fail to strike from the
horse of theological complacency those who would see us as the
pinnacle of creation in the traditional way.

There are of course the most profound theological implications, most of them well outside the scope of this chapter. But one
of the most immediate, and of the greatest importance in respect
of an environmental ethic is this: if other creatures have been created with the same loving care, the only position open to believers
who know their biology (just as surely as the believer who understood Galileo had to abandon a geocentric view of the universe),
is to look upon them, and act towards them, with a respect that
mirrors the fact that they have been brought into being with all
the care that has been lavished upon us, and that they share our
complexity on every level, differing only in detail. If other creatures have been created primarily for God's own fulfilment, then
our relationship with all creatures, and in particular the way and
degree in which we make use of them to serve our merely human
ends, and our attitude towards them, must be utterly infused with
the light of that reality.

What is new about this reverence for life — in contrast, say,
with that which has arisen from a deep human instinct and to different degrees in such religious groups as Jains and Hindus, or in
individuals like Francis of Assisi — is that the solid foundation on
which it is grounded is not instinct or revelation, but science.

The very same science which has unfolded for us this picture
of life is the same science to which we entrust our very lives every
time we board a plane or indeed throw an electric switch. It is a
perspective as well-founded as the conclusion that the earth is

round and not the centre of the universe. But science is not to be thought of in its primary meaning as a profession, a job carried out by people in laboratories. At its most fundamental, it is part of the essence of being human, not something that we don as a mantle (or a white coat): it is the use of understanding and intelligence, the most human thing there is in us. In this fundamental sense science is the exercise of our God-given body, mind, and spirit in pursuit of a fuller understanding of creation. It is in its most fundamental sense the exercise of the best of what we are; this is what distinguishes us from other species, and what gives us, ultimately, such power over creation.

What the practice of science is in its most fundamental sense is the unravelling of God's primary revelation through the use of the most precious of the natural gifts which he has bestowed upon mankind, namely his capacity to bring reason and judgement to bear upon his ever-expanding experience of the world and the wider universe of which it is such a tiny part. As such, it has added enormously to the depth and richness of our appreciation and understanding of what the word of God, speaking through his creation, is. Science is deeply rooted in the western tradition: but the new environmental ethic which develops from it is not to be framed within the narrow confines of a particular culture, for like the scientific tradition on which it depends and out of which it grows, it transcends these. That scientific tradition itself may have undergone its main development in western society, but that is an accident of history and fortune: one could almost say that had climatic history and geographical endowment been different it might equally have undergone its initial flowering in China or Africa or South America.

For those who profess belief in God, this establishes the most profound ethical imperative, because it demands of us a code of behaviour that relates to creation not merely as revelation, but indeed as an indissoluble part of our very relationship with God. Creation is part of who we are, of who He is. Nor can a dividing line be drawn in this regard between the actual living species and the inanimate environment of water, soil and rock they inhabit.

Life permeates everything, breathes everywhere: the whole, in this sense, is alive, interconnected and inter-related, and the ethical imperative therefore extends to embrace ecology. In John Muir's words, "when we try to pick out anything by itself, we find it hitched to everything else in the universe".

It may take a long time, but in due course this perspective will infuse the way all people of faith view the world. It is inevitable because science allows no other way of interpreting our relationship with Creation, once we add God to the picture. And because it may take a long time, it may be that by the time that understanding becomes the norm for the way the believer articulates the environmental ethics of Faith, we will have reduced nature's glorious diversity to a shadow of what was given to us in the Garden of Eden at the human dawn. We may find ourselves standing beyond the outermost gates of paradise, the clanging of the inner Cherubim-guarded gates still ringing in our ears, knowing that this time the flaming sword which turns each way, "to keep the way of the Tree of Life", has been conjured into being by ourselves alone.

The deepening appreciation that science has brought is fundamental to the patrimony of all humanity, and the sharing of that patrimony should be a priority for human action: so that the outlook of all may be enriched. The exercise of reason through science has enabled us to change the world beyond the imagining of earlier generations. It has provided us with the resources and techniques to make life better. But these resources have largely been channelled to make life better for me and mine, rather than for the human community as a whole, and certainly not for the great majority who have most need of it to enable them to reach a stage of development where their humanity can find itself; and not for the rest of creation, over whose backs we scramble in our urgency to maximise our own advantage. Our inability to apply the fruits of science in human affairs in a holistic way, or to share with others the achievement in understanding itself, demonstrates a failure to extend the exercise of reason beyond the narrowest of ends or to bring to bear on it the ethical informing that blossoms as wisdom.

Because the environmental ethic that a scientific analysis has given birth to is common to us all, it is something that should be an empowering bond between all communities of faith, of whatever tradition, something upon which they can establish a powerful and potentially enormously effective platform of action to break the impasse brought about by the brake that holds back the fuller flowering of reason as wisdom. In recent years, several thoughtful observers have advanced the view that the ends of environmental conservation will never be attained without the support of religion.[18] In the process of raising awareness of the values inherent in natural diversity, the churches have therefore a potentially pivotal role to pay. Of course, where arguments about the importance of sustaining natural diversity are put forward, it is the material benefits (especially the new genetic possibilities, and all those hidden cures waiting to be discovered) that are emphasised: and many commentators argue the need to emphasise the material usefulness of biodiversity in any campaign to secure its future, because of the essentially selfish and short-term concerns of most people.

Because communities, markets and politics are driven by the short-term imperatives of human society rather than the long-term cycles of nature, there is little likelihood of a solution to the environmental problems we face that is either strictly political or economic, the preservation of natural diversity among them. Short-term survival and improvement are our driving motivation, whatever the long-term costs, and it is here that the ethical dimension comes in. Two of Edward Wilson's books close with chapters arguing the critical importance of developing an environmental ethic.[19] Max Oelschlaeger has argued that "there are no solutions for the systemic causes of eco-crisis, at least in democratic socie-

---

[18] Feehan, J. (2002), "Biodiversity and Ireland — meeting the challenge of the Convention" in F. Convery and J. Feehan (eds.), *Achievement and Challenge: Rio+10 and Ireland*, 23–28. UCD, The Environmental Institute.

[19] Wilson, E.O. (1984), *Biophilia*, Cambridge, Harvard University Press; and (1992), *The Diversity of Life*, Cambridge, Harvard University Press.

ties, apart from religious narrative".[20] He argues that religion is
the only form of discourse widely available to Americans that expresses social interests going beyond the private interests articulated through economic discourse and institutionalised in the
market, and that for most Americans an environmental ethic will
either grow out of their religious faith or will not grow at all. In
his view, and that of many others, religious discourse is seen as
perhaps the most promising way to expand our cultural conversa-
tion to include non-market values such as sustainability, and to
revive citizen democracy.[21]

Of the relationship between science and religion, Stephen Jay
Gould — who was not a religious believer — nevertheless strongly
advocated that "these two domains hold equal worth and necessary status for any complete human life; and [although] they remain logically distinct and fully separate in styles of inquiry, however much and however tightly we must integrate the insights of
both magisteria to build the rich and full view of life traditionally
designated as wisdom".[22]

As we know in other spheres, religion can shape the political
agenda through its influence on the vote. As Oelschlaeger points
out, any mainstream religious denomination influences the nor-
mative choices of more people than all eco-philosophies put together.[23] And in recent years, a number of congregations within
the Catholic Church are beginning to see in the Care for Creation
focus the seeds of a new apostolate, with a particular awareness of
the social issues with which it is so entwined. This is especially
timely at this point in their history, where the State has embraced
most of the work for which they were originally founded, and
they are in the process of re-assessing their role in society.

---

[20] Oelschlaeger, M. (1994), *Caring for Creation: An Ecumenical approach to the Environmental Crisis*, Yale University Press, p. 5.

[21] Ibid., p. 12.

[22] Gould, S.J. (2001), *Rocks of Ages: Science and Religion in the Fullness of Life*, London, Jonathan Cape, pp. 58–9.

[23] Op. cit., p. 42.

10

ENVIRONMENTAL DESTRUCTION: THERE'S NO NEED TO FEEL GUILTY JUST YET

Richard Douthwaite

In common with almost everybody in the world, we in Ireland have yet to accept that the preservation of the natural environment is an ethical issue. We think it might be but that is as far as we can bring ourselves to go. It is true that the Green Party, by stressing inter-generational equity with slogans like "We don't inherit the world, we borrow it from our children", has tried to make it one. Fr Sean McDonagh has tried too, presenting the care of God's creation as a religious and a moral duty in his five pathbreaking books.

But while neither the sacred nor the secular message has gone unheard, they have certainly gone unheeded. Indeed, the rate at which the Irish are helping to ruin the planet has more than doubled over the past ten years, the result of this country's phenomenal economic growth.

So, if we heard the messages, why didn't we change our ways? Was it because we, like all humanity, are fundamentally flawed? Some people certainly think so, but in my view they are wrong when they put the universal failure to reform down primarily to greed and argue that, if everyone became less selfish and started to live in a state of voluntary simplicity, the destruction would stop and humanity could live sustainably on the planet for ever.

As long as the Earth supports more than a billion people, less lavish lifestyles for the wealthy will be an inescapable part of any effective arrangement to ensure environmental protection. However, there are two serious problems with a voluntary "Live simply, so that others might simply live" approach. One is the time that it would take to bring about the necessary changes in our behaviour: the other is the question of whether it is actually possible for people to live in a simpler way without bringing an economic collapse upon themselves. Let us look at these in turn.

First, the timescale. All the world's major religions have been trying to make their adherents less selfish and greedy for centuries and yet our over-consumption has still plunged us into a sustainability crisis of unprecedented severity. How long would it take our moral mentors to get us to cut our consumption sufficiently to defuse the rapidly deteriorating environmental situation, even if they redoubled their efforts at persuasion and were backed up by the media and the schools?

And how long can we give them to do the job? A decade at most, judging from the timetable we have to meet to deal with the most urgent environmental problem facing humanity, the threat of climate change. In the course of the century just ended, emissions from the burning of huge amounts of fossil fuel caused the world to warm by about $0.6°C$, and 2002 was the second warmest year since 1856, when widespread record-keeping began. The 2,000-plus scientists who comprise or advise the International Panel on Climate Change have concluded that we dare not risk average global temperatures rising by more than a further three degrees Celsius because, if they do, the world's forests would begin to burn uncontrollably — exactly as has been happening most years in Indonesia since 1997. The fires would release huge amounts of carbon dioxide, the main gas causing climate change, and set off a runaway warming.

Even if we stay under the three-degree limit, wind speeds will increase and violent storms become much more frequent. There is also a risk that the warming already in train will prevent the water in the Gulf Stream cooling sufficiently to sink to the bottom of the sea off the coast of Iceland in order to return to the southern oceans. If it does, the climate in the northern hemisphere could cool by as much as 10°C in as little as ten years and give Dublin a climate equivalent to that of Spitzbergen. In short, global warming presents a very real threat of a catastrophic, irreversible climate change taking place in the space of a few years. This change would kill a large proportion of humanity, and many animal, insect and plant species would become extinct.

Keeping below the three-degree limit means keeping the concentration of carbon dioxide in the atmosphere from rising above 450 parts per million (ppmv) — the level figure is about 370 ppmv today, up from 270ppmv in 1750 before fossil fuels began to be burned on a large scale. To stay below the 450ppmv ceiling, we have to start reducing our emissions within the next ten to fifteen years at such a pace that, by 2050, they are down to half the current level and reach no more than an eighth of the present rate by the end of the century.

Nobody believes that moral suasion *alone* — and I stress alone — can bring such a massive transition about in so short a time, although it could certainly help enormously in creating a supportive atmosphere in which the legal, economic and monetary frameworks required for such a shift could be built. Moreover, once the frameworks are in place, the fact that we feel that they are ethically right will make them marginally more effective. However, our morality will not matter much at that stage as most of us will comply with them because, as with income tax legislation, they will have been designed to allow us no alternative. Ethical considerations will simply grease the wheels and sugar the pill.

Let us move on and consider the second problem: can we achieve anything worthwhile by trying to live more simply in today's world and, if we can, could we do so without causing an economic collapse? The fact is, the way we do almost everything these days is extraordinarily complex and we have lost the means to make it simple. How about digging a hole in the ground? A straightforward job with a pick and a spade, wouldn't you say? Well, not any more.

Towards the end of the 1950s when I was still at school, I thought that I might like to become a civil engineer. My father arranged for me to spend my summer holiday working as a junior engineer with a firm of contractors connecting the houses in a village outside Canterbury to a new sewage system. One day a short, broad-shouldered Irishman arrived at the site office wearing an immaculate but — for the period — rather flamboyant suit. He had come to price digging the trenches through people's gardens to the main sewer in the road outside. His men would do the job entirely by hand. "You should see these gangs of Irishmen work. They really go at it hard. They can make a lot of money but they earn it", the site engineer told me.

A few days later, however, a new machine arrived on the site to show what it could do. It was the first JCB that anyone had ever seen. That was when the task of digging a trench became complex, because now it involved not just a pick and a spade but the whole process of first making the JCB — tyres, hydraulics, engine, gearbox, generator, battery and all — and then supplying it with fuel, which in turn required tankers and refineries and oil wells in the Middle East. I never heard whether the tanned, squat Irishman's gang got the contract but in any case, their days of doing things in a simple, direct, low-energy way were numbered.

Or consider the making of a cup of tea. Nothing simpler than that, surely? Certainly not a habit incompatible with a simple, sustainable style of life, one would think. Well, William Cobbett thought differently and he might have been right. He mounted a virulent attack on tea-drinking in 1822 when it began to displace beer as the daily drink of ordinary folk. Apart from its effects on health (he claimed it "rendered the frame feeble and unfit to encounter hard labour or severe weather") he was worried about the complexity of brewing it — all the time and equipment the process took and the fact that it required the lighting of, he estimated, at least a hundred extra household fires a year. Today, though, it appears that things have changed and it is just a case of switching on the kettle and then pouring the boiling water over a tea bag in the pot. But that apparent simplicity is an illusion. The making of tea is many times more complex than it was in Cobbett's day because it now involves, in my case, coal mines in Australia, a power station on the Shannon, a procession of pylons carrying high tension cables to a substation outside Westport, and from there a line of poles across the fields to a transformer about fifty yards from my house.

So, short of moving to somewhere remote to live in a community that still meets most of its needs directly from its own resources, there is no way that I can live simply in today's world. And what work would I do in a self-reliant community anyway? If I still wrote for a living, my earnings would continue to come almost entirely from the complex world. To claim I was living simply would therefore be a sham.

"Ah," I hear you say, "he's twisting the word simple. 'Living more simply' doesn't mean not relying on complex systems. It means living more frugally, consuming fewer resources, living on less."

All right, I agree, but I wanted to stress the complexity of the way we live now to make this point: complexity is always associated with high levels of energy use. This means that almost regardless of how we live in today's Ireland, although we might not be directly responsible for it, we are occasioning a lot of fossil energy use. Moreover, our present way of living is going to be hard to maintain if we decide to restrict our consumption of fossil energy to keep our greenhouse emissions down.

In any case, suppose that I do cut my spending and, with the things I continue to buy, I choose as far as possible those that are produced in a less resource-intensive way. I get my car repaired again and again, for example, rather than having it replaced. Repairs and hand-made goods can cost a lot but let us assume that I am successful and that I cut my expenditure by, say, twenty per cent and that this leaves me with money in the bank at the end of the year. What then? Well, the bank's job is to take any money its customers save and lend it to customers who wish to borrow. Consequently, if the bank can find a borrower, the fact that I have

saved merely releases the resources I would have used to someone else. The net benefit to the environment is nil.

Even if moral suasion works and lots of people cut back their
spending simultaneously, the result would be much the same. The
fall in consumer demand would leave many firms with excess capacity. They would therefore cancel any new investments they
might be making and that would threaten a great many jobs. This is
because in a modern economy, somewhere between 16 per cent
(Sweden) and 27 per cent (Japan) of the labour force is employed
on projects which, it is hoped, will enable the economy to grow the
following year. Up to a quarter of a country's workers could therefore find themselves made redundant and, with only their savings
or social welfare payments to live on, they would be forced to cut
their spending too. This, in turn, would cost other workers their
jobs. The economy would enter a downward spiral, with one set of
job losses leading to another, a decline that it would be very difficult to reverse.

The prospect of anything like this happening terrifies governments so much that whenever a shortfall in consumer demand
seems to be developing they cut interest rates to encourage people
to borrow to spend more. Normally this strategy works but if it fails
to boost the economy, they increase spending themselves. They feel
they have no option but to do so because the consequences of an
economic contraction are so severe. Growth must continue whatever the social or environmental damage it might cause.

Japan provides a very good case history of this. In the late
1980s, the Japanese economy boomed. Land and share prices
doubled in the space of three years and a general inflation seemed
likely. To head the latter off, the Bank of Japan decided in 1989 to
force its citizens to do exactly what the "live simply" advocates
recommend. It put up interest rates both to make everyone consume less and save more. The policy worked only too well. As
Japan has an aging population, more people wanted to save for
retirement than to borrow. Moreover, millions of them had run up
huge debts in the boom years and wanted to pay them off. Accordingly, saving soared and by 1993 the economy had ceased to

grow, very few private-sector investments were being made, and the rate of inflation was heading towards zero, a level it reached the following year.

"Consume faster or it will gain on us!"

Source: Ted Trainer (1989), *Developed to Death*, Green Print, London.

Having overdone the demand reduction, the government was forced to begin spending more itself to prevent widespread unemployment. It borrowed the money to embark on massive, and frequently totally unnecessary, public works projects. As a result, dozens of under-used roads, bridges, ports and airports now litter the country and the amount Japan owes in relation to its national income has become so large that the scope for further state borrowing is restricted, particularly since the credit-rating agencies reduced their grading of Japanese government debt to below that of Botswana in 2002. But even this spending was inadequate to stop unemployment gradually increasing. The present joblessness rate is over five per cent, a very high figure for Japan, and the social distress it is causing is immense.

The unfortunate truth is that, in our present system, an individual cutting his or her consumption back has no effect and if we reduce our consumption collectively, the state is going to feel bound to increase consumption itself — if it can find the money to do so — to prevent an economic disaster and mass unemployment.

Happily, there is something worthwhile individuals can do instead of cutting back: they can switch their expenditure away from imported goods sold in chain stores to locally produced ones sold either directly by their makers or through locally owned shops. They can also move their savings to a credit union or a fund that invests in their area — putting money into a normal commercial bank or pension fund simply strengthens the money-must-grow system that is the main culprit for the damage being done. Admittedly, the environmental benefits of both steps will be tiny but those involved will be planting the seeds of — or helping to preserve — the locally based economies that will be an essential element in a sustainable future.

My conclusion from all this is that, since we cannot achieve anything worthwhile to protect the Earth within the time left to us either by acting alone or in a voluntary relationship with others, caring for the environment is not a matter of individual morality and no-one should feel personally guilty about what is happening. Collective measures backed by legislation are needed to protect the planet. Billions of individual ethical decisions will never suffice.

The ethical issue facing us as individuals is therefore not so much the number of brownie points each of us scores for the simple style in which we live but about what we are doing personally to promote a systemic change. This is where the real choices lie and thus the morality. Buying imported organic food through a supermarket or a smaller car is only fiddling around at the edges. They are ways of kidding ourselves in order to feel good. They are, in fact, just another form of consumerism.

We urgently need to develop an economic system that would permit growth to stop. One which would allow us to say "Ireland is now one of the richest countries in the world. It does not need to grow any more. In fact, it simply must not grow, because the resources our growth consumes are required to raise living standards in the desperately poor parts of the world and by future generations." We do not have this option at present and until we do, protecting the environment is not a moral question.

The climate change crisis puts the growth issue centre stage. Cutting our greenhouse gas emissions and hence our fossil energy consumption by around 5 per cent a year, the sort of rate required to stay within the three-degree Celsius limit, will mean not just that growth in industrialised countries stops, but that their overall levels of output sink. A research project directed by Professor Olav Hohmeyer at the Centre for European Economic Research, Mannheim, in 1998[24] showed that it would be possible to reduce the fossil fuel consumption of the fifteen countries in the EU at the time to zero by 2050 at the cost of shrinking the average incomes of their populations to 84 per cent of their then level. On the other hand, the number of jobs would increase.

Other studies have produced similar results. Professor Malcolm Slesser[25] found that if Britain ceased generating its electricity from fossil sources and used only renewable sources instead, its material affluence would fall. The construction of nuclear reactors was necessary if economic growth was to continue. However, because fossil energy would be required to build the reactors and to provide their fuel, carbon dioxide emissions continue to rise under the nuclear scenario. Indeed, they would fall off only slowly under a no-growth, 100 per cent renewable energy scenario, because wind turbines and photovoltaic panels also require fossil energy for their manufacture.

What this means is that, as nuclear power will not help us to reduce our carbon dioxide emissions, continued economic growth is incompatible with preventing climate change. That is, unless some novel, environmentally benign source of energy can be developed. That might never happen and, even if it does, it would not be of much benefit for at least two generations because of the time and resources required to put it into place on any significant scale.

---

[24] LTI-Research Group (ed.) (1998), *Long-Term Integration of Renewable Energy Sources into the European Energy System*, Heidelberg: Physica-Verlag.

[25] Malcolm Slesser, Jane King and David C. Crane (1997), *The Management of Greed*, Edinburgh: Resource Use Institute.

Since most economic growth results from higher levels of energy use, this raises moral questions. All of us have niggling doubts about the fairness of a global economic system which enables us to use a lot of energy and live in prosperity while millions of others use much less energy and have to get by on less than a dollar a day. Up to now, we have attempted to resolve these doubts by saying to ourselves, "If we can get the poor countries' debts wiped off and open our markets to their goods, and if we can increase the rich countries' aid budgets, then their economies will start growing and they can enjoy prosperity, too."

This was never a particularly convincing argument, as we all knew how many planets it would take to provide the resources for everyone to live at the US level. Its merit was merely that it was the only justification around for continuing with the current growth-based system which, after all, is the only one we know. But once we accept that humanity has grossly exceeded the limit to fossil energy use set by the planet's capacity to absorb greenhouse gas emissions, even this "Growth will help the poor catch up" fig leaf disappears. We can no longer escape from recognising that the limits to the Earth's capacity to produce sustainably are currently being exceeded. If we restrict production to get back within the limits and then take more than our fair share of the reduced output, others will have to accept less.

Further economic growth in Ireland inevitably involves our increasing our pollution of a global commons — the atmosphere — in order to increase our output. Malcolm Slesser has calculated that, each year, half a typical country's fossil fuel consumption can be necessitated by its attempt to grow. So the collective challenge before us is to find a way to change the way the economy works so that this country can stop growing without suffering an economic collapse. But what is there that we can do about that as individuals? Here are my suggestions:

- Refuse to vote for any party that advocates continued economic growth.

- Make it clear to politicians that, as growth is no longer an option, you are prepared to see your purchasing power fall to, say, 1992 levels, so that the poor can be made better off.

- Press the government to set a timetable for the complete phasing out of fossil fuels over the next fifty years and insist that it gives Sustainable Energy Ireland or some other agency the budget to make it happen.

- Join Feasta, the Dublin-based Foundation for the Economics of Sustainability, which is one of the few organisations anywhere developing strategies for weaning the world off growth. See www.feasta.org

- Find out about the Contraction and Convergence proposals for an international framework for the reduction of greenhouse gas emissions. These allocate emissions rights on an equal per capita basis and have been accepted by a majority of the countries of the world. See www.gci.org

- As we discussed, buy locally produced goods from locally owned outlets as often as you can.

Nothing you can really get your teeth into, I'm afraid, because the required reforms to the economic system involve changes in the way that money is put into circulation. Very briefly, these involve abandoning the use of money created when people take out loans at the bank and replacing it with money which is spent into circulation by the government. The problem with debt-based money is not just that its supply shrinks if people become reluctant to borrow, creating a recession, but that the amount of borrowing has to increase year by year to enable interest to be paid. This means that the economy has either to grow or to inflate to enable the burden of debt to be contained. A hurried explanation, I'm afraid, because the reforms are outside the scope of this article, but you can find more details on the Feasta website.

Everyone should be able to play a role later on, however. As I write, the world economic system is slipping into a depression

that will probably turn out to be at least as deep as that in the
1930s. Only armaments spending during the Second World War
brought that to an end. During the war itself, a determination
grew up that, after the conflict was over, the system that had
brought it about must not be restored. Herbert Read, who wore
many hats but is perhaps best known as an art historian, wrote a
poem, *To a Conscript of 1940*, about the way that his generation,
that of 1914, had failed to prevent its re-emergence twenty-five
years earlier.

> We went where you are going, into the rain and the mud,
> We fought as you will fight,
> With death and darkness and despair;
> We gave what you will — our brains and our blood.
> We think we gave in vain. The world was not renewed.
> There was hope in the homestead and anger in the sheets,
> But the old world was restored and we returned
> To the dreary field and the workshop, and the immemorial feud
> Of rich and poor. Our victory was our defeat.
> Power was retained where power had been misused
> And youth was left to sweep away
> The ashes that the fires had strewn beneath our feet.

Similarly, the challenge presented by the coming depression will
be to ensure that the system that caused it, one which has shown
itself to be highly unjust and environmentally unsustainable, is not
restored afterwards. Power must not stay where it has been mis-
used — with the big nations, with the institutions they control like
the World Bank, the IMF and the World Trade Organisation, with
the money men and with the giant corporations. An alternative
must be developed that returns power to localities and to billions
of hands. It is here that the local economies I mentioned will play a
part. And while these are being built up, a climate of opinion must
be created in which the return of the old regime comes to seem totally unacceptable. In both those activities, everyone can choose to
play a part. If some do not, well, it might not matter. There will be
no need to consider where the guilt lies unless the rest of us fail.

11

TOWARDS AN ETHIC OF INTERDEPENDENCE: A PERSONAL VIEW

Trevor Sargent TD

I believe in miracles. I believe in resurrection. I also believe in the interdependence of all life.

Every day, the realities of miracles, resurrection and interdependence are brought home to me at home in Balbriggan as my wife Heidi and I prepare food looking out at our vegetable garden. The apple cores, stalks, peelings and general food leftovers are all collected in a newspaper-lined large bowl kept under the sink. When full, the bowl is emptied into the compost tumbler outside. The miracle is to observe how food leftovers become food delights for millions of microbes, earthworms and other fascinating soil dwellers. In a matter of weeks in summer or months in winter, those food leftovers and the lining of newspaper have been transformed into earthy, friable, black compost. That in itself would be miracle enough — but to grow the healthiest and tastiest of fruit and vegetables in soil reinvigorated by this compost is a manifestation of the miracle which is life itself.

Over the years, experience has taught us that the best compost and hence the healthiest vegetables and fruit come from the widest diversity of organic matter. A mix of newspaper, grass clippings, kitchen leftovers, pigeon manure, cut nettles and comfrey work together far better than just one or two of these ingredients.

This cherishing of natural diversity has reinforced my belief that, similarly, diversity of cultures, races and ethnic backgrounds in human society is not just healthy but essential for the health of society as a whole. The analogy with composting also cautions me that no one ingredient or culture should be so dominant as to overwhelm all the others.

The dominant and oppressive position of humanity in relation to other species illustrates this point. In October 2002, the World Conservation Union admitted that only four per cent of plant species worldwide have been classified, yet 5,714 of these plant species are threatened with extinction. Since 2000, another 121 creatures have been added to the Red List of Threatened Species, bringing the total endangered to 11,167 species. Clearly an ethic of interdependence is needed to ensure decision-making (whether it be personal, governmental or global) is not genocidal, ecocidal and ultimately — knowing our dependence on biodiversity — suicidal.

Gandhi said: "The greatness of a nation is to be judged on the way it treats the most vulnerable." Gandhi included people and animals and all life, however marginalised, in that maxim.

The challenge of Gandhi's measurement of greatness requires strength and wisdom in such quantities beyond the limitations of human abilities that for me, a spiritual dynamo is a prerequisite for ecological change. This reality keeps me close to my own spiritual dynamo, Jesus Christ, and each time I break bread with fellow Christians, I say the following words: "Let us work for all people and indeed all species marginalised and upon whom we are all interdependent and whose marginalisation or indeed loss makes all of us poorer and ultimately more vulnerable." And to quote from 1 Corinthians 10:16–17:

> The bread which we break is a sharing in the Body of Christ. We being many, are one body for we all share in the one bread.

12

THE CHURCH AND A JUST SOCIETY

Gordon Linney

MORAL MALAISE

It may seem a strange thing to suggest that Ireland, in a period of unprecedented prosperity and achievement, faces danger. At a time of momentous change within the island of Ireland and in our status within Europe, the stability of our key institutions is critical. Instead, there is an inherent instability resulting from a loss of credibility in church and state, extending to the professions and business community.

It does not end there. There may be widespread anger at revelations of corruption in high places and allegations of false election promises but this has to be qualified in that the credibility issue goes much deeper. The reality is that the comfortable classes monopolise the political franchise in this country and because they are materially well looked after they vote in a particular way, motivated by self-interest and with very little thought for the common good and especially for the disadvantaged. Moral concerns are hardly to the forefront where politicians with serious question marks over their conduct can be re-elected by fawning constituents, in some cases with increased majorities.

We have a democracy but it is a conditional democracy, a democracy of the contented and the comfortable and therein lies the

real danger for the future good and stability of this country.
Surely alarm bells ring when the independent Rowan Charitable
Trust declares:

> Ireland is now the most corrupt country in Europe. Tradi-
> tional notions of integrity in Irish public life were battered
> by a succession of tribunals which revealed patterns of cor-
> ruption at the centre of Irish politics, administration, public
> life, education and banking, accentuated by political crony-
> ism.

Somehow the churches escaped — or were overlooked.

INTEGRITY: A CORE VALUE

It is not necessary to make a case for the importance of *integrity* in
public life. It is self-evident and speaks for itself. It is a key element
in that body of baseline values which give cohesion and shape to a
nation or any institution if it is to earn and retain the loyalty and
commitment of its citizens or members. Without *integrity* there can
be no authentic scheme of justice or sense of fairness.

This can be seen from the impact of recent scandals affecting
corporate America. The collapse of major business corporations
such as Enron had enormous and tragic consequences not only for
the employees who lost jobs and savings but also for the international economy and millions of people whose pension funds and
other investments were hugely devalued. Business confidence
was shaken to its foundations in an instant. Why? Because of a
moral failure. Individuals and professions that were assumed to
be trustworthy proved not to be.

We should note the speedy response of the American authorities by way of judicial proceedings and new legislation and compare it to the situation in Ireland where too often political interests
take precedence and conceal things or try to slow them down.

This raises questions about the party system. It is true that
most of the people engaged in politics in this country are honest
and decent. But they are often compromised by the fact that their

first loyalty is to the party. At one level, one can understand the need for such loyalty and the compromises that go with membership but what of those occasions when there is a conflict between the national interest and the party interest or a choice to be made between what is right and what is wrong? In the Dublin planning scandal, it was an octogenarian assisted by a firm of solicitors outside the jurisdiction who brought the issue to the fore. What does that tell us about politicians and the legal profession here?

Of course one recognises that politics is the art of the possible. At times it is a game between parties in which achievements will be exaggerated and problems minimised, depending on which side you are on. Moral principles and political strategies are sometimes uncomfortable bedfellows.

Truth like love is a many-splendour'd thing but there are parameters within which we have to operate if public confidence is to be sustained. It is arguable that in the past ten or fifteen years we have crossed the boundaries of what is tolerable even in politics but there are still signs that some people at least prefer it that way.

THE STATE OF THE NATION

Political credibility has been seriously undermined following the 2002 general election. It was clear, to those who took the trouble to enquire, that there were mounting financial problems. The ESRI and several respected commentators were quite specific about the state of the public finances but somehow the issues never came to the surface. Smart talk and slick presentational skills full of wild promises did what they were intended to do. They made enough of the electorate feel comfortable. There was no mention of higher electricity charges, increased health charges, college registration fees, secondary school fees and reduced funding for educational disadvantage, third world relief and much else. To compound the offence, the electorate was told after the event that they knew what they were voting for.

There is an air of contempt and a frightening arrogance in that attitude. One is reminded of Marie Antoinette and her cake. Someone, somewhere has to say stop for the sake of the country.

If this were a once-off glitch it could be put down to experience but in the lengthening shadows of the Flood Tribunal and other inquiries, there appears to have been a golden circle of converging political and commercial interests, not yet fully exposed, who worked the system to their own advantage with little accountability to anyone. Some businessmen did whatever was necessary to make money. Some politicians did whatever was necessary to gain power. In the process many were hurt and disadvantaged. The worrying question is, has anything changed?

Corruption is an extreme consequence of the loss of integrity in any walk of life but there are others less obvious. For example, there is emerging in what is often called today "good" government an increasing tendency to avoid responsibility, to place accountability on someone else's desk. This can be seen in the way health boards, hospital boards and even school boards are placed in the firing line of public anger and frustration when things go wrong or do not measure up to people's expectations.

This is especially true of the health service where doctors and nurses are under enormous pressure. The government and the civil service at the centre have budgetary control and therefore real power. But when things go wrong, responsibility and often blame is placed on local management and their professional colleagues working with limited resources.

Good government will tell the public that there are limits to what we can afford and that they cannot have everything they want in a health service unless they are prepared to pay for it. Instead we are given nonsense undertakings that waiting lists will disappear in two years.

THE MIND OF THE CHURCH

Whenever a churchman enters a debate of this kind, he will inevitably be told the church should not be involved in politics. Bishop Desmond Tutu when challenged on this invited his questioner to show him what version of the bible he was reading! Politics have been defined as "that part of ethics which relates to the regulation and government of a nation or state for the preservation of its safety, peace and prosperity". How can the church not have views on such matters?

Inevitably, there are those who prefer a "privatised" religion, which can lead to a "privatised" and undemanding morality with strict parameters within the cult. They would identify with the immaculately dressed inner-city curate in *Strumpet City* who loved the altar but preferred to socialise in Kingstown. Not so his old parish priest who could not detach himself from the lives of his people or close his eyes to their poverty and distress. He knew that Christianity is an incarnational religion linking life and faith. Whether we like it or not, it involves dealing with the things that belong to Caesar as well as God.

In his book *The Christian Priest Today* (1972), Michael Ramsey, Archbishop of Canterbury wrote:

> There is a tendency of religious people often to picture themselves a God who is supremely interested in the religious aspect of life . . . and is less interested in the drama of human life itself. He is the God of the temple and scarcely the God of the factory and the farm, the sciences and the technologies, and millions as they go about working and earning. Is it not true that the image of God can be seriously distorted in this way in the attitudes of devout people?

The language may be dated but the message still holds for the churches in Ireland struggling with a process of change that is both disturbing and challenging. Economically, we are being internationalised; politically we are being Europeanised; and culturally we are being pluralised and to a great extent secularised. Until the second half of the twentieth century, the churches were part of the establishment with real power derived from their roles as providers of services in schools, hospitals and other agencies. That has changed significantly and will continue to change.

In this process of change, the churches are being forced to re-examine their position against a background of declining numbers and diminishing material resources. It would be easy to settle for the *God of the temple* and let the world go by but that would be to abandon the prophetic role of the church, a role powerfully represented by such people as Mother Teresa, Martin Luther King, Archbishops Desmond Tutu and Oscar Romero. Their work in a variety of ways courageously asserted human values and dignities where people were degraded and devalued and where principles of equity and justice were ignored. It placed them in a state of healthy tension with the secular powers. In some cases that did not come easily but it was forced upon them by the exigencies of the day and the moral convictions that were basic to their own lives.

Oscar Romero was by nature a conservative man who as Bishop of Salvador tried to control his more radical clergy who were opposing a corrupt government. He was a reluctant hero but was left with little option following the murder of one of those priests. He became their champion and was eventually himself murdered. In 1980 when receiving the Nobel Peace prize he said:

> The church has committed itself to the world of the poor. The words of the prophet of Israel still hold true for us; there are those who would sell a just man for money and a poor man for a pair of sandals. There are those . . . who fill their houses with what they have stolen, there are those who crush the poor.

This awareness of the prophetic role of the church in society has always been a source of tension in the Judaeo-Christian tradition. Prophets and priests did not and do not always see eye to eye. Dom Helder Camara, a great champion of the poor, once remarked that when he gave food to the poor they called him a saint. When he asked why the poor have no food, they called him a communist.

Our situation in Ireland is not nearly as critical as that faced by Romero and the others but it is still serious and dangerous. Serious because for too long senior churchmen have walked the corridors of power and some still prefer to be part of the establishment. Dangerous because there are growing numbers of people, both urban and rural, who feel alienated from the political process and the churches. Apart from the work of CORI, it is rare to find a clear and focused comment on moral issues which gets through to people other than those dealing with marriage and human sexuality, matters deemed to be "moral". There is total silence about the abuse of political power and patronage; virtual silence about the greed of some and the indifference of many to the poor. And when statements are made, they are often non-specific and bland, other than through a few lone voices. There is a failure to recognise that the challenges facing Ireland today are not merely political and economic but moral and many people are longing for the leadership that the churches can and ought to give, who long to be affirmed in the values that they hold. And there is a failure to communicate beyond the church building and their ageing congregations to challenge younger people about the kind of society they are building.

Some will say the churches have been compromised by their own failures in such matters as clerical abuse, sectarianism and previous unhealthy political alliances. "Who are they to preach to others?" There is truth in that, but there is also truth in the fact that having failed, having been humbled and found wanting, the churches have learnt something of the costliness of moral failure and the loss of credibility. Gospel values are not diminished by the fact that all of us fail to live up to them. Furthermore, enough religious and lay have led and still lead the way in frontline areas of human need and deprivation.

Archbishop Robert Runcie, addressing British Parliamentarians in 1982, said:

> The church has a special concern to speak for the vulnerable, the inarticulate, those who are weak in bargaining power — for all those in our country who are at the bottom of the heap. It also has a concern for justice. This will mean that on, for example, racial questions, and on many matters of economic and social concern, it should have special things to say. If it fails to say them, it is not being true to its beliefs.

In Ireland there is a tendency only to see the marginalised in less popular groups like the Travellers, asylum-seekers or addicts of one kind or another. This makes it easier from a conscience perspective to walk away and to abrogate our concerns for them. But the marginalised include a vast range of people with needs and responsibilities such as the sick, elderly, carers, the disabled, the educationally disadvantaged, and many more.

In a country that still claims to be Christian, the churches have a right and a duty to challenge a too-comfortable electorate about the values and attitudes that inform their political decisions and how these affect others. There can be little doubt that current thinking encourages politicians to opt for social and economic policies that favour the better-off and impact harshly on the disadvantaged. Changing the attitude of the electorate will change the political agenda.

And the churches have a special responsibility to address those in power, not in a spirit of judgement or condemnation, but in a spirit of partnership. We need to challenge the love of power and money, which so easily leads to corruption in church as well as state, and promote the love of country and people that expresses itself in unconditional service.

A JUST SOCIETY

There are many ingredients to the *Just Society*. Here are three that need to be underlined in the Ireland of today:

1. **The Dignity of the Person.** From a Christian point of view, this is the assertion of a worth and dignity conferred by God on every human being. (Others hold the same view but from a different philosophical point of view.) Implicit in it are basic human rights such as the right to the necessities of life, the right to justice, the right to freedom of thought and belief, the right to live in peace and safety.

2. **Equity.** This has to do with the ordering of society and our treatment of persons within society. Equity is not to be confused with equality, which in the diversity of our humanity is

almost impossible to sustain. Equity has to do with fairness and the way we relate to and treat each other. It has nothing to do with who you know but everything to do with what you are as a human being.

3. **Positive Discrimination**. A truly just society is not a community of condescending handouts but a community of entitlement where everyone is treated on the basis of his or her needs and rights. Inevitably some will need more help than others because of some social disadvantage or other impediment.

CONCLUSION

It would be wrong to end without acknowledging the many good things that are part of our national life today. The various governments, the churches together with many of our other great institutions have combined in the past to enrich our way of life. But it is the people themselves who have achieved most by their sense of good citizenship, their sound values and hard work.

Events of recent years, however, have impacted negatively on this sense of the common good and created a different climate. Politicians either by misconduct or silence and inactivity have brought their profession into disrepute. Their credibility is seriously undermined and people will say quite openly that they do not believe them.

Some members of the business community and key professions such as accountancy, banking and the law have not only brought discredit on themselves but have shaken a public confidence that had taken generations to establish.

We in the churches have also to face the fact that in too many instances we have failed to live up to the standards and practices that we commended to others. We have failed many as a result.

The era of the Celtic Tiger has created an expectation, even greed, in a significant number of the people that there is always going to be more for them at no extra cost. The effect of all this has been a general disaffection with those in positions of power and leadership by growing numbers of our people, especially in the urban areas, who feel undervalued and effectively disenfranchised.

Leadership has been defined as the art of bringing people to a place where they have not been. For us a truly inclusive society where everyone counts is a place where we have not been for a long time, perhaps never, and to get there we need leadership at all levels that can be trusted and respected.

It takes us way beyond the resources of image-making and spin-doctors. It is about substance, it is about integrity. Are we up to it?

13

TEACHING MORALITY
IN THE CHURCH TODAY

Bishop Christopher Jones

CHRISTIANITY AND CULTURE

There are fundamental moral values on which all societies depend; for example, respect for truth, for justice, for the sacredness of human life and the unique dignity of every human person. Christianity, which has been the bedrock of western civilisation, is guided by values that are rooted in Scripture and especially in the life and teaching of Jesus Christ. Christianity has not only been part of western culture, it has been a formative element of that culture throughout history.

THE CHALLENGE OF SOCIAL AND ECONOMIC CHANGE

Urbanisation and industrialisation have had a huge impact on the culture of our people over the last two centuries. England and the US had a century to adjust to the impact but Ireland had to cope with the challenge in a few decades since the industrial revolution hit our land in the 1960s.

Thirty years ago, I worked in a New York parish. One evening I spoke with teenagers about their faith and their moral values. They had one moral guideline in their lives: "You can do anything you wish in life as long as you hurt no one." The values of the Gospel, the dignity of the human person, the sacredness of human life, the right to life and all the essentials for life — honesty, justice, integrity, forgiveness — had no place in their concept of right and wrong. The norms and customs, traditions and values of their family and local community had no influence on their lives.

NORMLESS VACUUM

The more I listened, the more I remembered Emile Durkheim, one of the founding fathers of sociology. He carried out the first ever piece of scientific research on human behaviour and his subject was suicide. In his research, he discovered that in times of rapid social and economic change, people and especially youth find themselves in what he called a state of "anomie" — a normless vacuum adrift from all the anchors of family and community which can be such a support in life.

I believe this is where the young people in New York were finding themselves, and that is where, thirty years later, our young Irish people are found. They are caught up in a culture which has been secularised over a few generations and which has no time or place for the spiritual dimension of the human person, for God, for Scripture, for Jesus or for his teaching on life and on death.

THE CHALLENGE OF THE CHURCH TODAY

The great challenge for the Church in every parish today is to help our people through prayer and study to rediscover God at the centre of their hearts, their homes and their communities. This challenge has been made all the more difficult by the scandals in our Church today. Since I became bishop in 1994, we have all been so shocked to hear story after story of sexual abuse and especially to hear that priests and religious have inflicted such suffering on children. I often think that if the Church had set up a Committee to design some means of damaging itself and its mission it could not come up with anything more damaging than child-sexual-abuse by priests and religious. It is so important that every possible effort is made to heal the sufferings of victims and bring perpetrators to justice. I honestly believe that the humiliation and suffering which we are all experiencing will give birth to a much more humble, caring, compassionate and transparent Church.

THE CHURCH IN THE LOCAL COMMUNITY

Thank God, despite the waves of anger generated by specific TV programmes the Church in the local community has remained very understanding and loyal. People in the local parish know their priests and know that their priests are with them on their journey especially in times of illness, loneliness and bereavement. While they are shocked by what they have heard, they can also see the efforts that are made to identify child sexual abuse with priests and religious. Local people are quite capable of perceiving hidden agenda.

THE RIGHT TO LIFE AND ITS CONSEQUENCES

As we read every day about more and more murders, suicides and deaths on the road, it becomes obvious that many people have lost all sense of the sacredness of human life. Add to this the continuing onslaught on the lives of the unborn and what all that is saying to us about concern for life.

Since ordination to the priesthood in 1962, I have always carried in my heart a deep and abiding awareness of the dignity of every human life. I believe that every human person is created in the image of God and redeemed in Christ. I believe that every human person is unique, distinct and never to be repeated.

I believe that every Christian is called through baptism to belong to the Body of Christ as a member of the family or community of God. I believe that every one of us is called every day to bring to our own brothers and sisters something of the love, the compassion and the forgiveness of God.

OUR SOCIETY AND THE SACREDNESS OF HUMAN LIFE

However, I have always been very disappointed and at times depressed by the way we as a society have treated our poor, our homeless, our alcoholics, our delinquents and others. We are happy to contribute money to good causes as long as our convenience and our comforts are not in any way disturbed. I see this especially in our relationships with Travellers. We are sorry for them. We do not like to see them suffer from the cold or from poverty. However, we know that there are one thousand families on the roadside without running water, toilets, electricity or litter-collection because of our prejudice. This money is available at Government level to provide adequate accommodation but most Government programmes have been frustrated by local opposition. I worked for eight years as secretary of the National Council for Travelling People and ten years as its Chairperson. I also served as adviser to the Minister of the Environment on issues relating to Travellers. All I can say is that if our treatment of Travellers over the years is any measure of our respect for human life there is great need for conversion in our lives.

OUR YOUNG PEOPLE AND THE SACREDNESS OF HUMAN LIFE

I do believe that if our young people could discover that God is the source of all life and that the dignity of every human person is rooted in sacred scripture, we would have far less murders, abortions and suicide in our lives and far fewer homeless families and individuals. Human Life is sacred and its destiny is beyond the grave.

Once we recognise and accept the sacredness of human life, we must also accept and promote the right to accommodation, education, health, recreation etc.

RIGHTS WHICH DERIVE FROM THE RIGHT TO LIFE

Ireland has made great progress in the education of the people at first, second and third level. However, it is so tragic that to date it has made no significant effort to give all its children equal opportunity at primary level. We all know that education is the key that opens the door of the prisons of poverty. Yet we see children coming to our primary schools year after year from homes where there is no education and where parents have no aspirations for their children's future in education. These children are sitting side by side with children who come from homes where their educated parents give them all encouragement they need. It has been said that "children of poor families enter the educational system with their hands tied behind their backs". Efforts are being made to promote remedial teachers in schools but these are little more than gestures to resolve a major social problem. Our people must be helped discover that children have a right to justice to the best of education.

RIGHT TO HEALTH

Again, once we accept the sacredness of human life, we must accept that every person has a right to the best available health service. And still we have such an unjust two-tier system operating in our society. Of course, as in education, it is the better off who formulate policies in health care and therefore they will be concerned essentially about those of their own socio-economic level.

OUR YOUTH AND OUR SECULAR CULTURE

The church must help our young people understand that while they have rights to life, accommodation, health, education, etc., they also have obligations to recognise and promote the rights of the poor and the marginalised.

They are born into a culture where economic and material progress and pressures have pushed God from the centre of hearts, homes and communities to the sidelines. It is not that young people and people not so young have conscientiously rejected Christ or the Church and its teaching. They are living in a culture where the pursuit of wealth, power and pleasure have no place for spiritual and moral development of the person. They live in a culture where there is no place for self-discipline or restraint of any nature on the independence or freedom of the person. Freedom without restraint leads ultimately to the survival of the fittest, the law of the jungle. Is this why the rate of delinquency, crime, violence of every nature, sexual abuse, rape, alcoholism, drug addiction, murder and suicide has risen so rapidly in recent years. Is this why tribunals have become so important in our country at this time?

MARRIAGE AND FAMILY LIFE UNDERMINED

One of the greatest tragedies for our day and indeed for the future of civilisation has to be the undermining of marriage and family life. Again one can see how all of this has grown out of a culture that seeks freedom and independence without any restraint or self-discipline. Couples claim to love each other and the children they bring into the world but are unwilling to make any commitment to each other or for their children. An increasing number of children are being denied their right to a father and mother for their growth and development. Of course many single parents make heroic efforts to prepare their children in love for life.

THE SCHOOL AND THE COMMUNITY

I have been convinced for a long time that parents and the community have thrown all responsibility for the evangelising of our people at our teachers and at our schools. Indeed, teachers are feeling more and more isolated because they experience such little support from parents, from the community and sometimes even from the priests. When parents give up on prayer in the home and on Sunday worship with the community the catechetical efforts of teachers are totally undermined.

A community, if it is a church community must recognise that it is called to care for its people. It must be a community where everyone experiences a sense of belonging, of being wanted, of being valued and of being loved. How can children experience a sense of being wanted, valued and loved if they ever experience a sense of community or of belonging to something bigger than the family or the school?

COMMUNITY

I believe that the greatest gift this Church can offer a cold and lonely world today is the gift of community. The Church is community from its origin, as illustrated in chapter two of the Acts of the Apostles.

It is in and through this small local community that young and old experience the love of God made flesh in the kindness of those around them.

THE COMMUNITY AND CHRISTIAN MORALITY

Jesus, who is God, became a human being and lived a life of love — love of the Father and love of the human family for which He gave his life. He showed His disciples that they too could live like this by following His example and He told them to make disciples of others. He not only taught them about God's love for them, He also formed them into a community where they learned to live and love as He did. An authentic commitment to Him is possible only within the context of membership of His community. So to live a moral life is to not a matter of rules and regulations but of forming a human community as disciples of Jesus. It is a matter of faith.

Michael Paul Gallagher SJ likens Christian faith to the first smile of an infant:

> For weeks you smile and express your love . . . then one day your baby smiles back. He or she has entered into a different relationship, has responded to all you have given. It is a moment of recognition, of love. Our life of faith is exactly like that in its core simplicity. God loves us in Christ and one day we must realise it . . . there is a danger of reducing faith to morality or to the externals of religious belonging. If that happens religion becomes a matter of "I thought" or "I ought not". Needless to say the commandments come alive and make best sense if God's love is received and recognised — like that first smile.

We are called into a personal love relationship with our God and, as in any relationship that matters to us, our decisions are about what will please the person we love. In the final analysis, morality is about relationships — relationship with our God, with each other and with our world, relationships that call us to be other-centred, to be concerned with the well-being of others, to grow in love. It is a lifelong process — every decision we make forms habits.

In the end, each one of us is responsible. Victor Frankl, a survivor of the horror of the Nazi concentration camps, says: "Everything can be taken from a person but one thing, the last of the human freedoms — to choose one's attitude in any given set of circumstances, to choose one's way." This is the freedom God gives us — the freedom to make moral choices.

CONCLUSION

Life is about relationships, not about things. The happiness of any person or community comes not from jobs, though jobs are important, not from homes, though shelter is important, not from cars, though transport is important. The greatest joy comes from good relationships — the greatest sorrow and suffering come not from loss of job or property but from broken and betrayed relationships. All relationships of love are rooted in the love God has for all of us. Christian morality is living in harmony within a community of love — a love that has its source and strength in the love of God.

14

WHERE TO FROM HERE?

Fr Harry Bohan

INTRODUCTION

Values are incorporated in international documents and in the mission statements of corporations. They are intrinsic to the nature of organised religions. Most people have a set of core values but the speed and excesses of modern life are such as to leave little time to identify what they are and apply them to real life. Furthermore, in many cases, from the global to the local they are too aspirational, theoretical and abstract. And they are swamped by the capitalist global value of the market. The market value has become the real religion of the western world, including Ireland.

Market values are central to business and commercial life but inappropriate when they over-influence certain professions — medicine and the law, for example — or when they exploit young people, push family life to the sideline and in general take over or swamp human and spiritual values.

There is no doubt that the past ten years of economic boom have brought undreamed-of material benefits to Ireland. In many ways, we never had it so good. But there is a serious unease. Events are bringing home to us that all is not well. We are uneasy about:

- *Family life*   Who is rearing the next generation?

- *Politics*   Could capitalism destroy political democ-
                       racy as people find that the market gives
                       them more power than the vote?

- *Spiritual vacuum*   Where is the sense of meaning coming
                       from?

- *Community*   The rise of crude individualism has led to
                       the breakdown of shared networks.

- *Poverty gap*   The faster an economy grows, the greater
                       the gap between rich and poor.

DEBATE

In November 1998, a few of us living and working around Shannon ran a conference entitled "Are We Forgetting Something? Our Society in the new Millennium". As Marie Martin from Omagh, one of the chairpeople, put it, it turned out to be "like no other" in many ways. The first day, she said, "brought together some of the finest speakers it has ever been my privilege to hear, and raised very high expectations — which were subsequently fulfilled — for the second and third day". The "Are We Forgetting Something?" Conference proved to be an unforgettable experience and eventually laid the foundations for the establishment of "The Céifin Centre" for values-led change which, among other things, runs a conference each year with a specific purpose of involving a cross-section of Irish society in a debate on the direction Ireland is taking. The papers from these conferences have been published.

I want to underline the importance of the debate. I am convinced that the current malaise about public life is inextricably linked to a failure by civic and other leaders to engage our citizens in a debate centred explicitly on values. You cannot capture hearts and minds with paperwork. It is not facts that mobilise a society, but the values animating them. If we diminish our ability to speak the language of values, we will soon lose the language.

Our society in Ireland and our community in Europe caught the imagination of their founding fathers because the values which necessitated their establishment were as plain and as obvious to them as daylight. They had experienced and lived through the alternative. Our society needs to return to the ground of values to begin the process of democratic, social, spiritual and economic renewal which is evidently overdue. We need to find a language and a method of doing this.

Whatever one's particular beliefs, it is fast becoming clear that the threat of dumbing-down civil debate into an eventual value–illiteracy would lead to an unravelling of consensus, community and solidarity in the years ahead. Indeed, if we continue to diminish our ability to speak the language of values, it is the atmosphere in which democracy and civilisation itself are nurtured which is at risk.

UNDERSTANDING CHANGE

Céifin is fundamentally about the rehabilitation of the core values of individuals, families, communities, corporations, institutions and organisations. It is about providing a counterweight to those of the marketplace. Its work begins *where people are* — in the home, workplace, the community and across the generations. Corporations, institutions, organisations, professions, are then challenged about their values and how they respond to the needs of the people.

We have found that the real problem is not that values have changed but that the values held can no longer find expression. Céifin puts a value on the people. It underlines the fact that understanding change is important if we are to manage the future. A significant element of that change is the fact that there is a perceived crisis in the ability of systems, as we have known them in the past, to deliver improved performance in key areas of life. There is serious growing disillusionment with government, with organised religion, with politics, and with business.

There are a few reasons for this, but maybe I should first try to put our current situation into context. Since 1958, and for very good reasons, Irish society has been busy constructing an economy. Prior to then, emigration had drained the life-blood from Irish society with 40,000 people emigrating each year during the 1950s. Prior to that again, we had experienced the rationing of the Second World War, the economic war of the 1930s, the struggle for independence and, of course, the Famine and its aftermath, which left an indelible mark on generations of Irish people. The Famine had a traumatic effect on the Irish psyche. Ireland lost half of its population in a few decades. The experience reverberated long after food was available again in steady supply.

I see the last century opening with colonialism, then dominated by clericalism and ending with capitalism. During all this time, community action was in many ways the one great buffer to the excesses or dominance of any one influence.

Against the background of all these influences — poverty, the fight for survival and independence and emigration — it is no wonder that the provision of jobs and building of an economy became a priority. The 1960s experienced the beginnings of major change in the form of an industrial, communications and educational revolution, which paved the way for our booming economy of the 1990s, when Ireland became the second biggest exporter of software in the world. As this New Ireland was being let loose, the old one was losing much of its shine.

RECONSTRUCTING SOCIETY — FROM WHERE PEOPLE ARE

That is a sketchy outline of where we have come from. One could ask where we are today; indeed one could ask what we, or anyone else, can add to the torrent of words in circulation. Our annual conferences and the work of Céifin are an attempt to read the signs of our times, to listen to the real concerns of people and to respond.

In material terms, many of us never had it so good and indeed many people feel good about life in Ireland today. However, the numerous tribunals and scandals have alerted us to a serious ethical/moral problem in the worlds of business and politics, but also in our everyday lives. Some people would even suggest we are living outside a moral/ethical framework. Many are confused, angry and cynical. We all know that we can only survive on the basis of trust, whether at home, school, work or in the community, and yet our society seems to be experiencing a fairly serious breach of trust. This leaves us with a huge challenge not just to identify the key issues but much more important to work out together what we can do about restoring trust. There is no need to dwell on those breaches of trust any further except to say that the scandals that have plagued modern Ireland with regularity in recent years are effectively the betrayal of the present generation by the preceding generation. They call attention to the civic nature of morality.

From our work in the Céifin Centre, we have come to a conclusion that we are not short of analysis or critiques in modern society. They don't tell us anything new and tend to be fairly repetitive. Our major challenge is to search for solutions, to take responsibility for our future and we believe that the reconstruction of society will take place from the bottom up. We need to be careful that in critiquing Irish society today, we are not satisfied with highlighting the problems. There is even a danger in this. These problems can often seem so vast and intractable that we feel powerless to enact any significant change.

So looking at values and ethics in Irish society today we believe that, at their best, systems cannot respond to the needs of people without underlining what those needs are and the only people who know their needs are the people themselves. A hierarchical church is not connecting to the spiritual needs of people; a school system is not touching the lives of growing numbers; the health system has become irrelevant to many; insurance companies are putting people out of business; and so on. These are examples of systems that worked in a stable environment but cannot work in a world that has become more complex, more interconnected, more global and less predictable. If we want proof of the failing of systems working on their own, we only have to notice that the people involved in the key public services — teachers, nurses, gardaí, even clergy — are becoming more and more vocal in their objection to directives which are not connecting with their own lived experience and that of the people they serve.

There is every indication that the twentieth century was the era of organised man/woman. Often though, our institutions became more important than the people they were designed to serve. They are now faced with the challenge of re-forming and reconnecting to the real needs of people.

TAKING RESPONSIBILITY

The modern western world defines itself through a number of rights: the right to information, the right to access, the right to know what is going on. But there are other even more fundamental rights. Children have the right to innocence. Young people have the right to grow up and we all have a right to trust. All of us have a right to expect good leadership — to look for leaders with two basic qualities: character and competence. People will accept tough medicine once they know they are getting the honest truth. Parents, politicians, teachers, bishops or corporate executives rank honesty as the single most important quality. However, they feel betrayed when their leaders are economical with the truth.

We also need to tackle a much deeper problem: there is a crisis in personal moral character at the grassroots level. We can so easily live in the comfort of talking someone else's story or scandal. These have to be dealt with truthfully, openly and honestly, but we must not allow ourselves to be over-cynical or feel too helpless.

We need to move on. Children will always need parenting, neighbours will need neighbours, people will have to take certain responsibility for their own lives and we will have to reconnect with ourselves, with others, with creation, with our Creator.

We feel that it is an appropriate time for people from a cross-section of society to come together to debate the place of values and ethics in our society to identify what difference each one of us can make and to take action. It is a time to put soul and community back into Irish life.

SPIRITUAL PERSPECTIVE

The answer to many of our current problems might be much simpler than we think. Our work is indicating to us that the crisis facing us today is not so much economic, environmental or political. It is a spiritual crisis. Any crisis, whether it is in the home, workplace or church, means that the old way is not working anymore. This is both a danger and an opportunity. The danger is that if we continue trying to find solutions with the old way of doing things, the crisis will not go away. The opportunity is to adopt a new way of thinking and acting.

It must be obvious at this stage, after a decade of extraordinary developments in material well-being, that wealth alone does not lead to greater fulfilment. As crime, alienation and social exclusion increase, bureaucracies respond to pressing issues in a short-term pragmatic way, using yesterday's procedures. Meanwhile, new laws proliferate, sometimes as a reaction to some obvious abuse. Most of the laws come without any serious debate or without seeming to arise from widely held values. As I write this, a law has been introduced to curb speeding on the roads. It is certainly having an effect, at least in the short term. But if we as a society do not value life — our own and others — to the extent that we will not misuse a dangerous piece of machinery such as a car, then the long-term effectiveness is questionable.

The solution or challenge is not how to create even greater freedoms in the world but to start looking inside ourselves to see how we can free ourselves. We in Céifin have come to the conclusion that the twenty-first century will be about the inner world or it will be about nothing. But there is a great need to provide space in our personal, work, home and community lives to identify our values. There is a need to pause and take a step closer to enlightenment.

CONCLUSION

Every culture maintains the existence of a soul. What is it? It is the existence of some kind of life-giving presence within all living things and within society.

We believe that the concepts of soul, community and shared values are vital for our future. These concepts are rarely discussed in a serious way. People are not comfortable in talking about them. They are seen as impractical or as being part of a particular religious tradition. In Ireland, many traditional values have been swept aside and people are being easily seduced into ways of thinking that market values alone will bring fulfilment.

There is an urgent need to develop a coherent set of values that can give us a sense of unity and purpose, a vision for the future and the ability to decide what quality of life we want for ourselves. We need to challenge the current ethic of personal material gain. If we don't, we will be faced with the slow erosion of our culture, through self-interest and greed. The values of community, co-operation and solidarity will fall into the background and we will continue to measure our progress as a nation only by crude quantitative measures. We need a new national philosophy which will put people and communities at the heart of our future.

15

ETHICS AND THE FAMILY

Gina Menzies

All happy families resemble one another,
but each unhappy family is unhappy in its own way.[26]

CHANGING FAMILIES

Families, when they live with mutual respect and harmony, create for their individual members an environment that encourages and sustains human flourishing. No state or institutional arrangement can provide for the same degree of human intimacy, essential for human growth and development, as the family: ". . . the family sets up the emotional bank on which we all draw for the rest of our lives".[27] This is not to deny evidence that many families fail in their nurturing tasks; some of the worst inhumanities that humans can inflict on each other occur behind closed family doors.

Our understanding of family and family life in Ireland has changed significantly in recent decades. Not so long ago, the norm of family consisted of a couple, who had married according to the laws of church and state, with children. The male partner

---

[26] Leo Tolstoy (1875–77), *Anna Karenina*, Chapter 1, p. 1.

[27] Paul Andrews (2000), "The View from Below — the Impact of Family Instability on Children", *Studies*, Summer, p. 107.

had the primary responsibility for providing the family's financial security, while the female partner was the homemaker and principal child-carer. Fathers were, in general, authority figures and decision-makers. John McGahern gave us a fictionalised example of such a father, drawn to an extreme, in *Amongst Women*.

Family patterns today are more complex and more freely constituted. Cohabitation, single parenthood, divorce, birth outside marriage, and women, in greater numbers, working outside the home, all challenge any exclusive definition of family. A family unit in the twentieth-first century, as described by sociologists[28], is a group of two or more people, related by blood, marriage or adoption, which lives together. Families exist more by choice than by legal or blood ties. It is impossible to give a catchall definition of family. It is more useful to refer to "families" than "the family".

ETHICS WITHIN FAMILIES

All families share common objectives with regard to family wellbeing, although how such objectives are worked out in each family may be significantly different. In the past, the traditional Irish family was referred to frequently as an *institution*. Its inner functioning was hierarchical and patriarchal. Decisions were made, usually by the father, on behalf of family members, and handed down, without reference to the needs or concerns of the member. Women and children were treated with the same lack of consultation about their interests.

Today's model of best practice in families is more open and democratic. Issues are discussed, information is exchanged amongst members, difficulties are negotiated and explanations given for suggested courses of action when dilemmas or conflict arise. There can be no blueprint for how families react to different situations and life experiences. But a template can be provided, which shows how to work through different aspects of family life. This is based on the model of family as a community of persons

---

[28] John J. Macionis and Ken Plummer (2002), *Sociology: A Global Introduction*, 2nd Edition, Prentice Hall, p. 436.

who respect each other, care for each other's well-being, and respond to each other's needs as they change along the path of life.

How families organise their internal affairs reflects their priorities and values. Families do not set out their ethical position in a formal manner. By their behaviour towards each other and their relationship with others who are not family members, they make an ethical statement about their fundamental orientation.

Justice and a democratic manner of dealing with all family issues represent the best ethical stance of a harmonious family community.

An ethic of care, guided by justice, creates the best environment for people of all generations to grow and to develop their full potential. Does the same ethic inspire and inform the Irish state's relationship with families in her guardianship?

STATE INTERVENTION AND FAMILIES

Historically, across all cultures, the family has been recognised as an essential value in civil society. Government interventions have sought to support family needs, at the same time keeping an eye on the needs of the state. Families with well-adjusted members make a positive contribution to society at all levels: this serves the interests of the state and also makes economic sense; there is a cost to the state in terms of finance and other resources, when families cannot fulfil their tasks.

Individual family members and the family as a unit in society have a variety of physical, psychological, emotional, educational and health needs. At the emotional and psychological level, families rely in general on their own internal resources. At the practical level, families depend, at least in part, on the State for support in organising accommodation, education, health and legal protection.

Government policies and legislation have profound impacts on families and their ability to carry out family tasks, especially the task of rearing the next generation. In China, the government's one-child policy created an environment where boy children were more favoured than girl children: not only has this led to many late abortions, but it has also led to an imbalance in the population structure. At the other extreme, Ceausescu's Romania promoted marriage to the point where a single person unmarried at twenty-five had to pay additional taxation. Even more interventionist was his population policy, which required every woman of childbearing age to have at least five children. This led to backstreet abortions: women established their pregnancy to comply with the law before having an unlawful abortion, which could be passed off as a miscarriage. On the other hand, French government policy of giving additional financial support to families with a third child has increased family size and ensured a replacement population.

ETHICAL PRINCIPLES AND GOVERNMENT POLICY

Legislation and government policy in family matters follow a vision of family, although this vision may not be explicitly stated. Where do we look for the ethical vision and principles that underpin Irish public policy about the family?

In the earlier part of the twentieth century, Irish government policy in relation to the family was based on the 1937 Constitution. This Constitution echoed everywhere Roman Catholic teaching about family matters, especially in areas of sexual morality and marriage.

In writing the 1937 Constitution, Éamon de Valera no doubt had in mind the traditional two-parent couple with children, married in the eyes of church and state. All Irish governments have recognised the value to the State of the family unit and the Constitution guarantees to protect this family unit.

Until the establishment of the *Commission on the Family* in 1995 (report published in 1998), Irish government policy has been founded on the guiding ethos that families should take primary responsibility for their own welfare.[29] Stated government aims and legislation in this area had not been based on any articulated vision of family. There was, however, an underlying presumption

---

[29] Mary Daly and Sara Clavero (2002), *Contemporary Family Policy*, IPA, p. 3.

that de Valera's ideal of the two-parent family, with the husband as the bread-earner and the wife as the homemaker and child-carer, was in the minds of the legislature.

The corresponding ethical stance was to preserve this ideal of family against all threats. Church and State were at one in their approach to family life. Divorce, contraception and women working outside the home were all non-contestable issues for both.

Partly because of specific constitutional challenges[30] brought by individuals, seeking to vindicate their personal rights and freedom in a democratic republic, Irish society and legislation have been forced to recognise different types of family groupings. Changes in relation to inheritance laws (1965), illegitimacy (1987) and social welfare codes have entered the statute book. Constitutional action was often the only route available to ordinary citizens to exercise freedom of conscience in matters that affected them personally and in a family context.

The 1937 Constitution and its articles on the family are the only formal statement where principles have been articulated which informed the State's policies on the family. Up to the publication in 1998 of the report of the *Commission on the Family*, there was no written source of principles in relation to the development of family policy. Even a brief glance at the Irish Constitution and its references to family is useful as an aid to understanding how an ethical stance on family informed legislation and public responses to family matters.

THE STATUS OF THE FAMILY IN THE CONSTITUTION

What can we learn of Irish legislation and the family as seen by the State? The State's role is delineated by the Constitution, and expressed by statute and regulations.

Articles in the constitution in relation to family matters cover recognition of the family as a fundamental unit in society, the position of mothers, marriage and education.

---

[30] For example, the McGee case, *McGee v Attorney General*, [1974] IR 284.

Definition of the Family

Article 41.1 of the Constitution states:

> 1° The State recognises the Family as the natural primary and fundamental unit group of Society, and as a moral institution possessing inalienable and imprescriptible rights, antecedent and superior to all positive law.
>
> 2° The State, therefore, guarantees to protect the Family in its constitution and authority, as the necessary basis of social order and as indispensable to the welfare of the Nation and the State.

However, the Constitution does not define *the Family*. It would be reasonable to surmise that de Valera, in framing the Constitution, had in mind the two-married-parent family as *the Family*. However, it is not what was thought in 1937 that matters, but rather what the Courts interpret. For example, in 1965, the Supreme Court held that a non-marital child could not be precluded from inheriting from her father's estate on intestacy. And the *Status of Children Act, 1987* removed in law the distinction between "legitimate" and "illegitimate" children.

Further, in practice, the State does recognise families other than the two-married-parent family. The Department of Social, Community and Family Affairs recognises cohabiting couples as being entitled to the same benefits as married couples ("A spouse means a husband, wife, cohabiting partner or a divorced husband or wife of the claimant."[31]), and lone parents are also entitled to benefits. So Government departments are stretching the traditional definition of *the Family* to include families other than those based on two married parents.

In essence, the State recognises that stable *relationships* are in the interests of society and citizens as a whole, whether these relationships are permanent or time-limited, conventional or non-conventional. Adequate finance is necessary to sustain any rela-

---

[31] Department of Social and Family Affairs website.

tionship, so by providing financial support, the State is attempting to promote the ethic of a stable relationship.

Full-time Mothers

Article 41.2 goes on to state:

> 1° In particular, the State recognises that by her life within the home, woman gives to the State a support without which the common good cannot be achieved.
>
> 2° The State shall, therefore, endeavour to ensure that mothers shall not be obliged by economic necessity to engage in labour to the neglect of their duties in the home.

However, the State has not followed the spirit of these articles in framing tax laws, which are at best ambivalent in their attitude to *the Family*. The "individualisation" of tax bands has been roundly criticised for discriminating against families in which one partner chooses to be a full-time homemaker. In this instance, it is clear that the Constitution is no longer the guiding principle behind taxation policy.

The state must restore the balance between work and family and give recognition to the spouse who stays at home. This does not necessarily require reversing individualisation. The Commission on the Family suggested a number of ways in which this could be achieved.[32]

Marriage

Article 41.3 deals with marriage:

> 1° The State pledges itself to guard with special care the institution of Marriage, on which the Family is founded, and to protect it against attack.

---

[32] *Strengthening Families for Life*, Final Report of the Commission on the Family, 1998, p. 168.

The original 1937 article was amended in 1995 to provide for divorce in limited circumstances. Legislation dealing with marriage breakdown is relatively recent, and recognises that the traditional two-married-parent family is not the only type of family. Legislation in this area is generally based on a non-judgemental approach, and the *Family Law (Divorce) Act, 1996* in particular seeks to protect marriage by making attempts at mediation a necessary prerequisite to the divorce process. The Commission on the Family recommends increased resources for mediation and suggests that the mediation services should be put on a statutory basis.[33]

Education

Article 42 recognises the role of parents as the primary educators of the child, but Article 42.4 goes on to provide:

> The State shall provide for free primary education and shall endeavour to supplement and give reasonable aid to private and corporate educational initiative, and, when the public good requires it, provide other educational facilities or institutions with due regard, however, for the rights of parents, especially in the matter of religious and moral formation.

Education has nearly always been understood to be academic education and vocational training. Despite the large sums of money expended by the Department of Education, many citizens reach adulthood without the basic skills of reading and writing. It is estimated that up to a quarter of the adult population cannot read and write at a basic level.

The concept of the family, with parents as the primary educators of their children, was the guiding principle behind government policies on education. Recognition of the partnership model of education, much talked of, has yet to seriously inform educa-

---

[33] *Strengthening Families for Life*, Final Report of the Commission on the Family, 1998, p. 226.

tion policy and initiatives. Following the recommendations of the Commission on the Family, new programmes in Social, Personal and Health Education, and Civil, Social and Political Education, have been introduced.

COMMISSION ON THE FAMILY

In recognition of the important role that families play in the state, the Coalition Government in 1996 established The Commission on the Family. The Commission published its report and recommendations in 1998. Since its publication, significant changes have taken place in government policy in family matters. This was immediately reflected in the establishment of the Department of Social, Community and Family Affairs.

This was the first occasion since 1937 that the state sought to reach an understanding of families in contemporary Ireland. An expert group was established under the leadership of Dr Michael Dunne. Its membership reflected social, legal, medical and economic expertise. It received the highest number of submissions ever made to a government commission. Research was commissioned and international models of best practice were examined in a number of relevant areas. It adopted an inclusive and wide-ranging consultative methodology.

The Commission's brief indicates a strong belief by the state that it has ethical obligations to families in its domain.

> to examine the effects of legislation and policies on families and make recommendations to the government on proposals which would strengthen the capacity of families to carry out functions in a changing economic and social environment.

The major thrust of the recommendations focuses on how government, through its policies and interventions, can support families in their multiple tasks, especially the task of being the primary carers and rearers of the next generation. It emphasised the need to co-ordinate family supports across a range of government departments and agencies, including the voluntary and community sector. A recommendation, immediately acted upon, was the establishment of a family unit within the newly named Department of Social, Community and Family Affairs. The function of this unit is to promote the co-ordination of family policy. Recently, this unit announced the setting up of a Forum on the Family to gather public ideas to feed into Government policy.[34]

At the beginning of the Commission's deliberations, the members acknowledged the need to establish principles to underpin the development of family policy. These are worth stating, as they represent the first articulation of an ethic guiding public policy on families in fifty years.

1. Recognition that the family unit is a fundamental unit providing stability and well-being in our society.

2. The unique and essential family function is that of caring and nurturing all its members.

3. Continuity and stability are major requirements in family relationships.

4. An equality of well-being is recognised between individual family members.

5. Family membership confers rights, duties and responsibilities.

6. A diversity of family forms and relationships should be recognised.

These principles, according to the commission, are essential truths about families. They mandate the State to base its relationship with families on an ethic of care, equity and justice.

The commission went on to make 44 recommendations. They cover every aspect of family life in Ireland today. Expert and accessible support for all family groupings is called for in every recommendation of this excellent report. The Family Affairs unit in

---

[34] *The Irish Times,* 21 December 2002.

the Department of Social, Community and Family Affairs is already influencing policy direction. One of the final recommendations from the Commission is a call for a Family Impact Statement as a means of routinely auditing the effects of proposals on families across all government areas. The Implementation of such a statement as well as the National Children's Strategy can create a much more inclusive framework for formulating government policy on families in the years ahead.

Many new challenges face families and government in our rapidly changing world. The issue of reconciling work and family life, care of elderly relatives and an increasing awareness of children's rights are already on the agenda. This agenda needs an ethical vision based on justice and care for all families that is open to new insights and inclusive of all its citizens.

16

THE ROLE OF THE FAMILY IN EQUALISING OPPORTUNITY

Kathryn Sinnott

I began to reflect seriously on the role of the family in equalising opportunity just after I had received a successful High Court judgment which had named and shamed the Irish State for inequality of treatment not just of my son Jamie and others like him but of myself and my family. Justice Barr's wise judgment rightly acknowledged the rights and shared welfare of the disabled and their families.

However, this judgment was subsequently appealed and I have been assured by the Irish Supreme Court that Jamie has passed the age of rights and that I as a mother, parent and representative of Jamie's family never had rights; and therefore no rights could have been transgressed.

That judgment has significantly changed my thinking in this area and causes me to offer three requirements for social change:

1. A change in the way in which we think about disability.

2. A removal of the many barriers which prevent people with learning disabilities from using ordinary services and participating in everyday activities.

3. A need to discover what kinds of support are needed to ensure that anyone with a learning disability really does have the same opportunities as their non-disabled neighbour.

Day after day, we deal with situations as they present. In the face of problems, action tends to be our activity of choice. However, when we find that despite all our action the problems do not go away and in fact worsen, it is time to take a step back and reflect.

There is wide public support for equality, as evidenced by the public reaction to the State's appeal of Jamie's case. If effort and goodwill alone could achieve equality, we should be seeing equality all around us, with many more of the barriers down and supports in place. We must be sure that the thinking behind our efforts is clear, consistent and acknowledges and fosters real equality.

The American Declaration of Independence states that it is "self-evident that all men are created equal". However, if the perception of someone encountering the disabled goes no deeper than what they see, equality will not be self-evident. We are not equally strong, able, attractive, wealthy, powerful, etc. The Irish Constitution gives us the answer to this self-evident equality, when it says that "all citizens shall, as human persons, be held equal".

So equality comes from personhood. Our equality is in our very existence as a human being possessing a human nature and therefore a human destiny. As Supreme Court Justice Murphy put it in July 2001, "It is that destiny which provides the logical basis for the constitutionally recognised rights of the individual."

This may seem very basic and obvious. It should also with a little thought be obvious that there is no other logical or consistent basis on which to believe in or seek equality except human personhood. If someone else can suggest a different basis for equality, I would be glad to hear it.

Equality based on human personhood is even obvious to those who deny equality to some persons. So obvious is it that in order to justify inequality and the denial of rights, word games must be played with the term "human person". Those who would deny equality alter the definition of human person, treating the term "human being" as a separate entity and referring to "human nature" as something that we aspire to rather than something we must possess. We saw these word games in Nazi Germany with the removal of "human personhood" from "human beings" who were disabled or Jewish. We saw it in South Africa where full personhood was denied human beings who happened to be black. And we see it today all around the world in the legalese that denies or seeks to deny personhood to some.

The next concept that is important to understand clearly is that the sole focus and reason for the existence of both the family and the State is the welfare of the human person. It should also be obvious that both family and State are made up of human persons. Unfortunately, as a direct consequence of the unwillingness to accept the self-evident meaning and implications of human personhood, states like the Irish State become self-serving. Increasingly, it sees itself as separate from and above the human persons who make it up and whom it is meant to serve. The State's shifted focus leaves the family alone to serve the human person.

To backtrack a little, the good of the human person is best served by striking and maintaining a balance. To describe this balance, imagine a tripod on which the well-being of the human person depends. The legs of the tripod are the individual, the family and the State. It is the responsibility and right of individuals to develop their capabilities and to fulfil their destinies as human persons. It is the responsibility and right of the State to foster the common good which is the well-being of human persons. Each has an inalienable, natural right to accomplish its function and a right to the means of accomplishing its function. The members of this tripod each has a right to respect and to non-interference in their function. They also have a duty to give support and even interfere when such assistance is needed.

The individual, the family and the State fulfil their functions in as far as they are able and should not usurp the work of the others. A young infant has a right to be fed and the family has a duty to feed the infant. However, when the child begins to reach out and grab food for themselves, the family must pull back and allow the baby to make the mess that learning to self-feed entails.

Since the object of a balanced tripod is the well-being of the human person, the requirement of a particular human person will affect the function proper of each member of this tripod. This is especially evident in the situation where the human person has a learning disability. For example, the learning disabled child may never learn to self-feed and it becomes the function of the family to feed her beyond the normal early months of infancy. If the family in turn requires assistance in feeding the person, it becomes the function of the State to assist the family. If the family becomes incapable of feeding the person, it becomes the function of the State as guardian of the common good to ensure that the person is fed.

So what is the "common good"? Here again, there has developed an altering of the definition which stems directly from the altered definition of human personhood. First, the real definition: the common good is a set of conditions under which human persons can fulfil their destiny. The conditions are:

1. Respect for the human person.

2. Social well-being and development.

3. Peace.

The Irish Constitution explains it in these words: "seeking to promote the common good, with due observance of prudence, justice and charity, so that the dignity and freedom of the individual may be assured, true social order attained . . . and concord established with other nations."

In the Sinnott judgment, Justice Barr explored the reasons for what he called the general malaise and widespread neglect of disabled persons. The reasons identified point to a pragmatic, possibly deliberate, acceptance of an altered definition of the common good. This altered definition equates the common good with a numbers game. Accordingly, the common good becomes merely the personal good of the greatest number.

Using this definition, it is reasonable to see resources spent on the education of a profoundly mentally handicapped person as wasteful because thirty normal children could be educated for the money or because the State could produce three PhDs for the price.

With a true concept of the person and of the common good, the profoundly learning disabled would be educated firstly because it was their right to fulfil their destiny and develop their capabilities as a human person and our duty as family and State to assist them. Secondly, they would be educated to promote social well-being and development or, in the words of the Irish constitution, "true social order".

So where does the family come in? In the area of learning disability, the tripod is definitely unbalanced and the family is in a unique and critical position. In the face of a deluded State, families and their supporters are often the only ones left to carry the torch of equality for the learning disabled person. The individual with a learning disability has at best a limited capacity to nurture and protect his own personhood. The Irish State, which should be attentive to the vulnerable, is not bothered and when pinned down talks about learning disability not in terms of persons but in terms of bigger or smaller slices of cake.

The family, as I see it, is all that is left to insist that human persons be recognised as equal. In the face of non-support and even obstruction from the State, families for the most part hold tough. Why? Because they have a bond of love and this bond allows them to seek the truth, to see beyond the disability to the valuable, vulnerable human person. The family bond makes them part of their child's struggle for development and dignity. No matter what the parents or family felt about the disability before it came into their lives, it is now personal to them. It has a face that resembles their own and a name which is the same as theirs. To the family, it becomes suddenly "self-evident that all men are created equal".

It is for this reason that families will move mountains and endure great sacrifice to remove barriers and put in place supports to open up opportunities for their learning disabled persons.

17

THE HEALTH SERVICE: ONE MOTHER'S STORY

Annie Ryan

I first became interested in disability issues when our eldest son, Tom, was not progressing as we knew he should. He was born in 1964 and could walk and looked perfect, but he could not talk. It was quite clear by the time he was four years of age that he had something drastically wrong with him. We brought him to the child guidance unit in the Mater Hospital and he was diagnosed as having autistic phenomena. The hospital authorities tried to get us access to some kind of service because they recognised that Tom was going to be very difficult for us to manage on our own but I remember them saying very forcibly, "Don't mention that he's autistic, whatever you do."

We lived in Sligo at the time and there was a big mental handicap centre just outside the town. We applied for Tom to get a place there. He was refused initially but eventually they agreed to take him on trial for a month in the mornings. At the end of the month, we were told "No way". I will never forget the sense of rejection; I felt that my son had been rejected and that I had been rejected. I happened to know the bishop at the time, Bishop Hanly, who was a lovely man and I told him what had happened. He said, "I can't believe it. That's why I brought them here. Will I make them do it?" One of the teachers from my son's school said, "No, you can't do it because all they will do is ignore him."

After that we tried to manage at home but Tom was disturbed all day and all night. We reached a stage where we could not cope on our own anymore and we were told there never would be the facilities we needed in Sligo. So we moved to Dublin. We got Tom into a school but only for a year. When the year was up, we were told he would not be taken back.

We went to a psychiatrist and he said there were no facilities for Tom in Dublin and advised us, "If he were my son I'd send him to the Rudolph Steiner school in Belfast." I remember the day we brought Tom up for the first time feeling that there was something strange going on — it was the day before internment was introduced. He was not the only child who had to travel to Belfast to avail of his constitutional right. Why?

After five years, Tom could not be kept in Belfast because he developed epilepsy and they did not have appropriate facilities to deal with this. There was no place in the state with appropriate facilities, so at the age of twelve, we sent him as a last resort to St Ita's in Portrane.

We decided, however, that we were not going to leave him there. We were going to find out exactly what was wrong with the system that people like Tom had to end up in Portrane. We met with parents and discovered there that was a large number of people around the country with a mental handicap who had nowhere to go except a mental hospital.

When Tom went to St Ita's Hospital in 1976 we stumbled on a scandal which had been going on for a long time. The conditions there, as in many of the mental hospitals, were appalling, and this was known to the people with the power to change them. Yet one never heard a word about them. Why was this?

The State had invested heavily in the general hospitals during the 1950s and the 1960s, at the same time grant-aiding the voluntary system. All this laudable activity was in stark contrast to the treatment which was thought affordable for the long-stay patients in the mental hospitals.

In the late 1950s, towns were proud of their hospitals. Every Sunday they were thronged by the visiting relatives of the patients and every day there was constant coming and going. During those same years, the mental hospitals stood lonely and unvisited, their isolation reflecting the rejection of their inmates by families and friends. It was a rejection that went deep into our society.

St Ita's Hospital had started out its long life as "Portrane Lunatic Asylum", built in the last years of the nineteenth century to relieve overcrowding at the other much older lunatic asylum at Grangegorman. The new Asylum was a vast undertaking. It was planned to accommodate some 1,200 patients. Sited on the sea coast and commanding magnificent views, it was a most impressive edifice. In the years since, little changed except its name. In 1925, it became known as Portrane Mental Hospital. In 1958, it shared in the general sanctification of the 1950s and was renamed St Ita's.

Close to the hospital were the wooden huts which had been used by the workmen who had built the hospital. In 1903 it had been decided by the joint committee which ran the hospital that they would retain those wooden buildings in case they were ever needed again. By 1904, one of the wooden buildings had been put into use again. All six were in use by 1966. There were 200 or so people with a mental handicap in those huts. Tom was just twelve, so he was in a children's ward which meant he was accommodated in the main hospital building.

At the time, it was very difficult to find out anything about St Ita's. Dr John O'Connell, a TD and medical doctor, had a special interest in this area, but when he visited St Ita's he was frog-marched out by two nurses without getting the opportunity to investigate anything.

A programme of refurbishment was completed in the early 1980s and the patients were finally moved out of the notorious huts in 1982. The newly refurbished units were an enormous improvement on the old festering eyesores, but the old mental hospital layouts survived. Mentally disabled people were still condemned to hour after hour in the large day rooms. They slept at night in the long dormitories. The numbers were still high.

In February 1982, at the height of a snow blizzard, the hospital was without electricity for a period of 31 hours. The generator at the hospital had broken down and so there was no heat or light. I understand that the nurses put all the patients to bed, sedated them and watched over them in their overcoats using torches for light. The newspapers were full of news of the blizzard and were particularly concerned about the plight of the sheep in the Wicklow hills. Not a word of what had happened at St Ita's ever reached the newspapers, although up to a thousand patients were involved. I was at home and was told what was going on. I tried to ring the Tánaiste, Michael O'Leary, because the Taoiseach, Garret Fitzgerald, was out of the country, but I could not get through to him. I rang up one of my neighbours, an army officer, and explained the situation to him. The following day, the army replaced the faulty generator.

It was in this manner that almost any progress in Portrane was achieved. After each crisis, usually involving some exposure in the media, one particular aspect of abuse would be addressed. This was a slow way to improve a service. It was particularly slow in Portrane, as the policy of emptying the hospitals, including St Ita's, gathered momentum. No effort was made to break up the over-large units. The minimum was spent on hospital maintenance. There was no attempt made to extend therapies to cover a larger number of mentally disabled people. Large numbers of people with a mental disability never left the dreary day rooms except to go to bed. As the Eastern Health Board put it in their report on the services at St Ita's Hospital in 1992:

> Since 1980 we have had an ongoing policy of transferring the less dependent residents from St Ita's. However, the vacated places were immediately filled by highly dependent patients, mainly disturbed.

In spite of the scandal of the huts and in spite of all the hopes of establishing a service appropriate to the special needs of the disabled at St Ita's, the hospital had retained its function as a dumping ground for the rejected people from the other services. As the Eastern Health Board put it:

> This has been largely to do with the fact that the emphasis has been on devoting the limited resources available to the needs of the less disturbed mentally handicapped . . . Most mentally handicapped persons with seriously disturbed behaviour invariably end up being admitted to St Ita's and become long stay residents.

I found no villains anywhere. On the contrary, one could not but be impressed by the hard work and dedication of those in charge of the services. How could so many honourable people, who were undoubtedly charitable and competent, allow such a situation to develop?

One answer might be that our political system, even our constitution, does not adequately protect the helpless, certainly if they are less than visible. And that prompts the most likely explanation of all: people want to sweep the issue under the carpet. The reticence with which the issue of mental disability has been approached does not help. When people have no voice, silence is not always golden.

Many thousands have died in the mental hospitals since the authorities ceased to pay any attention to reports on their conditions. It is right that we should remember them. For those people who died, well within living memory, the only fitting memorial would be the determination that such a state of affairs should never happen again.

Tom is thirty-eight now. The worst thing is that some people are still going through what we went through with Tom thirty years ago. I met a woman two weeks ago whose nineteen-year-old daughter was sent back to them from a "special school", and there is nowhere left for her but St Ita's, Portrane. All around Ireland there are parents with disabled children who are asking the question: what will happen to my child when I die?

POSTSCRIPT

As if to confirm the contemporary relevance of Annie's assessment, on 2 August 2000 the Inspector of Mental Hospitals, Dr Dermot Walsh, issued his Report for 1999. He referred to the, "generally unsatisfactory standard" of St Ita's and drew attention to the fact that the hospital was "under stress" because it provides for several hundred learning disability patients.

While the picture that emerged was one of slow progress, the report pulled no punches in its comments on a number of other hospitals. In one Leinster hospital, "The whole situation in the admissions unit was intolerable and could not be condoned". Almost a third of the patients in the hospital had "an intellectual disability and required specialist care in an intellectual disability facility" and "were inappropriately placed". Parents were, "not satisfied with aspects of privacy and dignity of care in the admissions unit".

18

WHEN SOME ARE LESS EQUAL THAN OTHERS

Finian McGrath TD

For all our talk of equal rights, a significant minority of people living in Ireland have not achieved legal, economic or cultural parity. The economic, political and cultural disadvantages suffered by these "outcasts" are serious violations of justice.

It cannot be disputed that the Ireland created by the Celtic Tiger is a much more prosperous one. Yet this creates dilemmas of its own. Contemporary society displays a proliferation of many interests, individual, social, environmental and medical, each demanding a fair share of society's scarce resources. Unfortunately, there are not enough resources available to meet all those needs. There is no easy ethical blueprint to which society can refer to establish that all of its obligations have been justly discharged. In the context of difficult decisions about the distribution of resources, awkward questions are raised. How is the tension between the rights of individuals and the overall good of society to be resolved? What are the relevant inequalities that justify giving more of the scarce resources to some and less to others? Clearly we require a balance between the rights of the individual, the good of the other and the common good: but how in the Ireland of 2003 are we to attain that correct balance? To date we are failing a significant element of our population. I have made this discovery through personal experience.

FAMILY TIES

Our second daughter Cliodhna has Down Syndrome. It was devastating for myself and my wife to Anne to hear the news after
Cliodhna was born. In the first 24 hours after her birth, it also
emerged that Cliodhna had severe physical problems. We spent
the first few weeks just wondering would she make it; once it was
clear that she was going to be physically healthy, we started to
focus on the other issues.

There is a massive sadness in any parent's life when they discover that their newborn child has a serious disability. The initial
reaction is: *Why me?* It was extremely difficult for the first six
months. After the psychological adjustment to the fact that
Cliodhna has Down Syndrome was made, we could not afford to
wallow in a dull fog of self-pity. The practical needs of our daughter's condition took over.

From day one, we had to fight and scream for every resource.
Our experience was that we didn't get the resources as a matter of
right. We spent years fighting every arm of the state to try to give
Cliodhna the best possible start in life. When she was younger,
Cliodhna kept our family very busy but not so busy that we did
not notice that there were huge inequalities and anomalies in the
way certain people with disabilities were treated. We began to see
what the conditions were like and they were horrifying.

I got involved in the Dublin branch of Down Syndrome Ireland and eventually became its chairman. That opened my eyes to
the scale of the problem on a national level. We have 2,000 members with Down Syndrome and they are all experiencing the same
problems with resources, or more accurately lack of resources.

A big issue for us was Cliodhna's education. We decided to go
down the integrated education route and place her in a "normal"
school for her primary education. She was in a class of thirty students and it was not until she was in fifth or sixth class that the
proper back-up services came on line, though her school was very
creative in how they used resources to meet her needs.

Cliodhna is fourteen now and we are very happy with the
education she is getting. We decided to send her to a specialist
school, Michael's House in Ballymun. A lot of parents, though, are

Michael's House in Ballymun. A lot of parents, though, are not so lucky and are on long waiting lists to get even minimal care.

WIDER QUESTIONS

For disabled people, the possibility of making decisions for themselves is often little more than a pipe dream. Decisions about their welfare are often taken by people who have no direct experience of what it is like to be disabled. The balance is shifting slowly, but the reality of disabled people participating actively in plans for their own rehabilitation remains far on the horizon. They are frustrated that the need for them to be consulted, and the importance of them expressing an opinion on the quality of the services which are being made available for them, does not seem to be fully appreciated.

In seeking a new deal for the disabled, it is important that this task is complemented with the establishment of adequate support systems for the families of disabled people. Many surveys suggest that there is considerable stress in the families of disabled people, particularly on the children. It has been claimed that the shock of being told that a family member is disabled is like being told that she or he has a terminal disease.

Much lip-service is paid to the disabled which fails to yield any practical benefits. Many medical and technical advances have presented new and exciting treatment options — the use of art and music therapy to help people cope with mental illness is just one such innovative example. However, there is a major shortage of funding which leaves many disabled people seriously disadvantaged. It is too easy though to talk about action for disabled people in terms of aspirations. What are needed are specific targets and specific action programmes.

This is not just an issue for parents with children who are Down Syndrome. For example, there are many people who are literally living lives of quite desperation because of a stammer. I know there are people out there whose lives have been shattered because they didn't get the help they needed. Young blind and visually impaired female pupils are being forced to travel to Northern Ireland for their education, due to the lack of facilities in the Republic. One student I know of is a fifteen-year-old girl from the west of Ireland who spends her weekdays as a student in Belfast, and is fostered on weekends because it is impossible for her to travel home every weekend. I find it incomprehensible that in this day and age such a situation is allowed to develop.

Despite the recent economic slowdown, there is plenty of money around and the amount of money that would be required to help people out in this situation is relatively minor and will not be a growing expenditure in the years ahead.

BIG ISSUES

A number of questions present themselves about the place of disabled people in 2003. In Irish society, are all people equal, or are some, like the disabled, seen as less equal than others? How many disabled people are institutionalised? How many have a home of their own? How many have access to the special education that they may require? How many have a job?

Successive governments have failed to provide the necessary infrastructure to support our more vulnerable citizens. Last year, the government attempted to railroad a Disability Bill through the Oireachtas and in the process demonstrated the utter contempt which exists in the halls of power for those requiring supports in this country. The proposed Bill did not include any rights for those with a disability. This same contempt has been shown time and again to carers, pensioners and those on waiting lists for a range of necessary hospital and specialist procedures. There is an ethical imperative that this situation must change.

ALLOCATION DECISIONS

When Imelda Marcos was first lady of the Philippines, she had a dream. She wanted to turn her country into the world capital for heart transplant operations — a perfectly admirable aspiration. The problem was that to achieve her ambition, she proposed to divert practically all her country's health budget to finance these state-of-the-art facilities. As a result, the budget for primary health care for the entire population would have been on a par with her personal budget for shoes. Her grandiose plans had to be shelved on foot of the tidal wave of outrage her proposal generated. It was almost universally accepted that treatment for the privileged few should not be at the expense of the impoverished many.

There is an ongoing tension in the health care system between what is the "right thing" economically and the right thing ethically. Successive Irish Ministers for Health boast about the amount of money that is spent on the health service. Although most civilised societies espouse the concept of the equality of all, this ideal rarely corresponds with the reality. Issues in the allocation of resources for and within health care are arguably the most difficult issues facing us today. As a former teacher, I am acutely aware that we also have huge allocation decisions to make in education if we are to ensure that our education system is to be an instrument of equality.

In health care and education, situations present themselves in which decisions must be taken and alternatives must be selected which will bring advantage to some and which may leave others disadvantaged. A political ideal, or a constitutional right might assert that every person has an equal claim to health and education but this aspiration is not always realised in Ireland; choices need to be made about which patients and which treatments will be given priority and which students will get to university. In a situation where there seems to be a contradiction in choosing some, in order that fair advantage may be given to all, then it is essential that we consider, however tentatively, the ethical grounds upon which choices may be made.

There is both an economic and ethical dimension to the problem of allocation. The basic economic problem is how society's scarce resources can be most efficiently allocated, in the light of economic facts and predictions, in order to satisfy human needs and desires. The key ethical dilemma is: by what means can we guarantee justice in the distribution of available resources? It is time we in Ireland had a more vigorous debate on this topic, in which the voices of users and carers are clearly heard and acted on. What kind of statement does it make when the government recently announced that it was spending €50 million to acquire a new government jet, and yet provided no funding this year for any new developments in the intellectual disability sector?

NEED FOR DEBATE

John F. Kennedy, shortly after his election as US President, claimed that the key issue of the modern times was the management of industrial society — a problem of ways and means, not of ideology:

> The fact of the matter is that most of the problems, or at least many of them, that we now face are technical problems, are administrative problems . . . [necessitating] very sophisticated judgements which do not lend themselves to the great sort of "passionate movements" which have stirred this country so often in the past.

His analysis has proven to be seriously defective insofar as philosophical questions continue to be crucially important in finding answers to many value-related issues.

To paraphrase Bob Dylan, the times are a-changing. As the old trees of established structures are dying, it is not easy to discern how to graft anew to the future vine. Ireland is at an in-between stage in its history, caught between a rich tradition and an as-yet unformed new direction. Violent crime is rising. Drug abuse brings havoc in certain communities. Traditional family life is disintegrating. The old certainties are gone. There is much confusion. The traditional answers seem redundant. New thorny questions occur with ever-increasing frequency. The vocabulary of right and wrong, of duty and the neglect of duty, of sin or shame has become difficult to use. In many cases, ethical choices do not occur in conditions where right and wrong are readily apparent, but rather the best decision must be wrenched from less than ideal alternatives.

Against such a backdrop, it behooves all of us in politics to provide the leadership Irish society needs if we are to create the just society that all our citizens deserve. We should all remind ourselves of Karl Marx's advice: "Philosophers have only interpreted the world. The point, however, is to change it."

19

IS GENDER EQUALITY AN ESSENTIAL FEATURE OF A JUST SOCIETY?

Deirdre de Burca

In this chapter, I will argue that any analysis of the extent to which Irish society is a just society at present must include an examination of the issue of gender equality and the extent to which contemporary Irish women enjoy the same status, rights and opportunities as their male counterparts. I believe that for too long our conception of a just society has reflected male norms and male preoccupations. A tolerance of persistent social, economic, and cultural inequalities between men and women is deeply embedded in our culture, and constitutes a serious obstacle to the achievement of a just society in this country. I will draw upon my own experience as a woman in Irish political life in an attempt to highlight some of the very real barriers that women encounter when they consider becoming involved, for example, in the male-dominated world of electoral politics. I will offer an analysis of why these barriers remain in place and explain how we as a society would benefit enormously from challenging and removing them. Finally, I will make some suggestions about how the gender equality agenda might be meaningfully advanced in this country.

I must begin by conceding that the social changes that have occurred in this country over the past forty years have certainly resulted in a dramatic improvement in the kind of freedoms and opportunities available to Irish women. The emergence of the feminist movement in the 1960s, and the implementation of progressive social legislation resulting from this country's membership of the EU, have meant that many former barriers to Irish women's social and economic advancement have been removed. Given the positive impact that these advances have had on Irish women's lives over the past few decades, it is often difficult to argue that we still fall far short of achieving true gender equality. Indeed, any attempt to make such assertions in the public domain is often countered by the charge that women are basically unwilling to compete on what is now considered to be a level playing field. Women who insist that considerable structural and attitudinal barriers to gender equality remain in place are generally viewed as strident feminists. Any suggestion that affirmative action may be required to help to redress the gender inequities that still apply in many spheres of public life is often interpreted as an attempt by women to achieve preferential treatment at the expense of their male counterparts.

Unfortunately, the Irish feminist movement appears ill-equipped to respond to these challenges at present. Much of the energy that animated it twenty or thirty ago appears to have dissipated. A considerable number of younger women who have benefited from the movement's campaigning activities appear reluctant to identify themselves with it, for fear of appearing extremist or anti-male. This broad trend has meant that the "official" Irish feminist movement has become less vocal and less politically influential, while the profile of its membership is ageing. The overall effect of the diminishing role and vitality of the feminist movement in this country is that the full implementation of the gender equality agenda has stalled. Many Irish women are aware that affordable childcare is largely unavailable in this country; that women's work in the home is unpaid and unrecognised within the formal economy; that paid paternal leave is unavailable for most fathers; and that female representation at the higher levels of management in both public and private sectors is unacceptably low. However, there appears to be a general sense of powerlessness or inertia amongst women in relation to tackling these issues. Key areas of public life including politics, business, sports, law and religion remain dominated by men. As a result, male norms, values and perspectives tend to inform activities within these spheres. Much of our public discourse, professional practice and policy-making is driven by male interests, and largely reflects male experiences and understandings.

In making these assertions, I am aware that I run the risk of being accused of polarising the gender equality debate and presenting a distorted feminist perspective.

I believe, however, that the proportional representation of men and women on decision-making structures within a given society must be a *sine qua non* of any model of gender equality being promoted within that society. Women comprise approximately 50 per cent of the population globally, and it is reasonable to expect that their views, priorities and experiences should be proportionately represented within decision-making processes that impact on their lives. The reality is that, though women have made inroads into certain spheres of public life, they remain largely excluded from important power structures and key decision-making forums, both nationally and internationally. One need only consider the overwhelmingly male composition of the UN Security Council as, at the time of writing, it deliberates on the threat of a unilateral US military attack on Iraq, or the almost exclusively male political leadership of the European Union, to realise that women's voices are largely absent from key international debates. Therefore I do not believe the views I express above are either biased or extreme.

The issue of the proportional representation of males and females within key decision-making processes is closely related to the question of whether the views, priorities and experiences of women are qualitatively different from those of men. This question is, to a certain extent, a contested one .The argument is often made that the interests of women do not differ in any significant way from those of men, and that the status quo serves women's interests as well as it does those of men. It is interesting to note that many who hold this opinion have also been critical of the feminist movement for what is seen as its determination to promote equal-

ity between the sexes by attempting to deny the essential differences that exist between men and women. In other words, there
appears to be an inherent contradiction in the logic of those who
view women's under-representation on public decision-making
bodies as unproblematic and yet who insist that there are fundamental and essential differences between men and women. I, for
one, fail to understand how the largely male composition of most
important public decision-making structures in this country can
ensure that women's interests are properly represented in the decisions that are made. I would be equally sceptical about the ability
of bodies with an almost exclusively female membership to make
decisions that adequately represent male interests. In my opinion,
the status quo is inherently unfair. The fact that as a society we are
often "gender-blind" and have become habituated to the extremely
skewed patterns of male over-representation and female under-
representation at most important decision-making levels of public
life, does not make these practices acceptable or right.

In an attempt to illustrate the point that I am making, I will
use the example of the under-representation of women in political
life in this country. When one examines how male power is institutionalised and organised within the political world, one is reminded of Weber's concept of "occupational closure". This refers
to the way in which a particular occupational group seeks to control entry to a trade or profession in order to preserve, defend or
promote its status and interests. Parkin (1979)[35] defined exclusion-
ary strategies of "closure" as involving the downwards exercise of
power in a process of subordination as a social group seeks to secure, maintain or enhance privileged access to rewards and opportunities. I would argue that the use of similar strategies of
"closure" by men ensures that politics remains a bastion of male
power, apparently invulnerable to the kinds of advances that the
women's movement has made in other areas of public life.

Whether at a local, national or international level, our politicians tend to conform to the simple stereotype of "men in suits".

---

[35] Parkin, F. (1979), *Marxism & Class Theory: A Bourgeois Critique*, London: Tavistock.

The vast majority of Irish political parties are "boys' clubs". The systems of patronage and cronyism that have established themselves within these parties tend to ensure the perpetuation of the "boys' club" at the expense of the few female politicians who have managed to penetrate the party's ranks.

Party leaders are almost inevitably male and this tends to influence the choice of successor. Selection conventions within the parties generally tend to favour male over female candidates. The culture of Irish political parties, and political life generally, is male, competitive and adversarial. The working hours of most politicians are very family-unfriendly and a crèche has yet to be established within Dáil Éireann for deputies with young children. The vast majority of political journalists and commentators are male and appear to take male politicians more seriously than their female counterparts. Political debates on radio and television programmes often feature a token female contributor, or sometimes none at all. Many male programme hosts appear unaware of the issue of gender balance when choosing the line-up for their panel debates, and members of the public have become accustomed to hearing serious political debate being conducted largely by male politicians.

The cumulative effect of these practices has meant that Irish women are deeply disadvantaged politically. Ireland's record on national parliamentary elections shows that the number of women elected is closer to the figures from sub-Saharan states than those of our northern European counterparts. Women's presence in the Dáil has risen by only 1 per cent in ten years. Ten counties out of 26 currently have no female TD. The number of women appointed to Cabinet decreased by 7 per cent for the current Government, while the number of women appointed as Ministers of State declined by 11 per cent. The percentage of women councillors has remained static at 15 per cent during the last decade and women have only a marginal hold on many other public and regional bodies.

Serious questions must be asked, therefore, about the representative nature of decision-making in this country at present. If women, who form half of the population of Ireland, are represented by only 13 per cent of sitting TDs, or if they rely for their representation on men, then the capacity of the existing political system to represent women adequately is seriously diminished. While it is often argued that conscientious male politicians can represent women as adequately as female representatives, women do bring a unique perspective to policy-making and decision-making generally. It has been found in the US, for instance, that women legislators are more concerned with women's issues and with issues related to families and children. When women make up a larger proportion of those elected at a national level, they are more likely to give priority to women's issues. This reflects a general consensus amongst experts that it generally takes a critical mass of women to effect change. It is generally recognised that such a critical mass is reached only when the percentage of women in parliament has reached 40 per cent.

According to the National Women's Council of Ireland's recent report *Irish Politics — Jobs for the Boys*,[36] the hidden barriers preventing many women from exercising their democratic right to become involved in politics are numerous. The barriers identified by the report include socialisation, incumbency, the under-representation of women in traditional entry-points, childcare and the lack of family-friendly policies and working hours. In relation to socialisation, the report refers to feminist academic work that suggests that girls and boys are reared to believe that politics is a man's game while girls are socialised to identify more with caring duties in the home. Research on British candidate selection indicates that women often perceive the roles of MPs to be largely based on typically male lifestyles and hence do not regard themselves as eligible.[37] As far as incumbency is concerned, the report refers to studies that argue that the low numbers of women in politics is due to the power held by existing office-holders (incumbents) when they are going forward

---

[36] *Irish Politics — Jobs For The Boys: Recommendations on increasing the number of women in decision-making*, National Women's Council of Ireland (2002).

[37] Joni Lovenduski (1996), "Sex, Gender and British Politics" in Joni Lovenduski and Pippa Norris (eds.), *Women in Politics*.

for re-election.[38] In US elections to the House of Representatives, for instance, over 95 per cent of all existing members won their seats in recent elections. A low turnover of elected representatives makes it even more difficult for women challengers to get elected.

The report also refers to the issue of the under-representation of women in traditional entry points and argues that another factor is that of occupational segregation and the low percentage of women in law and business, traditional stepping-stones into politics. As far as childcare is concerned, the NCWI report argued that one of the principal barriers to a career in politics for Irish women is the absence of childcare supports. The report suggests that many decades of Government inaction have led to the development of a childcare crisis, which restricts women's opportunities to combine paid employment with family life or to engage in time-demanding career choices such as that of politics. Where family-friendly policies are concerned, the report suggests that considerable progress will need to be made in this area to provide adequate supports for women to reconcile work and family life effectively. It is pointed out that while parents in Ireland are entitled to fourteen weeks' unpaid parental leave, those in Germany receive three years' paid leave, in Austria, two years' paid leave, in Sweden, eighteen months, and in Italy, ten months. The absence of adequate family-friendly policies are viewed as making it almost impossible for parents of young children, particularly women who bear the more considerable caring role, to enter a career which is demanding, insecure and where the hours are not family-friendly. As far as family-unfriendly working hours are concerned, the report argues that the pattern of long working days when the Dáil is in session prevents many women with children considering a career in politics. Long parliamentary sessions lasting into the night were explicitly cited as the reason why many women Labour Party MPs decided not to go forward for re-election in the UK in 2001, even in safe constituencies where they were certain of re-election.

---

[38] Joseph F. Zimmerman (1994), "Equality in Representation for Women and Minorities" in Wilma Rule and Joseph F. Zimmerman (eds.), *Electoral Systems in Comparative Perspective: Their Impact on Women and Minorities*.

The overall conclusion of the NWCI report was that proactive action by Governments does bring about an improvement in the percentage of women elected at local and national level. Quotas have been found to be very effective in Sweden, where they were implemented across party lines and at a high enough level (40 per cent) to bring about a significant improvement in the number of women elected. A similar result was obtained in Norway and Finland. In Denmark, a comprehensive gender equality policy supplemented the quota mechanism and helped to boost women's participation in politics. However, in France, the rate of change as regards women's representation was considered to have been most remarkable. France has significantly improved its formerly low level of women's representation through the introduction of a parity law that is accompanied by financial penalties if parties fail to comply with the parity requirement. The number of women councillors has increased from 21.7 per cent in 1997 to 47.5 per cent in 2001. The percentage of women senators has increased by 5 per cent in three years. The NCWI report calls on the Irish Government to draw on the French model to introduce legislation to bring about parity democracy in Ireland, to require political parties to introduce a quota of 40 per cent of women candidates for national and local elections and to make 50 per cent of funding for parties dependent on their compliance with this requirement. The mechanisms for improving the participation of women in political life therefore are clear and specific. What is still lacking is the political will necessary to bring about these changes.

Those who despair of the possibility that women will ever achieve parity of representation in political life should reflect on how unlikely it must have seemed two hundred years ago that women would succeed in emerging from the domestic realm into the economic and political world of men. For women, getting into the workplace, becoming workers and earning their own money has proved a necessary but insufficient step towards liberation. Many would argue that a further but necessary condition is for men to move the other way, to get into the home, to start nurturing, to participate more fully in domestic life. Considerable cultural and social barriers exist to prevent men from playing an equal role with women in the domestic sphere. These barriers largely reflect a paradigm of hegemonic masculinity (i.e. men as dominant and powerful) that has had considerable currency within our society over centuries. This paradigm is premised upon the idea of a bipolar maleness/femaleness, or an understanding of men as opposite to women. The cultural and social practices shaped by this paradigm serve to sustain the false polarity. Men dominate the public sphere while women's strengths tend to find expression in the private — usually the domestic — sphere. A number of feminist writers have spoken of the "entrapment" of male and female roles and of the obstacles in the way of realising an egalitarian ideal as far as men and women are concerned.[39]

The emerging politics of gender identity, however, has interrogated many of the assumptions underlying popular conceptions of masculinity and femininity. It is contended that the meanings of masculinity and femininity are not fixed but rather the dominant definitions of normal masculinity and femininity have largely been shaped by white, male, western, middle-class, heterosexual views of the world. Within this frame of reference, the supposedly passive, co-operative, nurturing, community-oriented and process-oriented female is seen to complement the active, competitive, aggressive, individualistic and task-oriented male. The attributes of the male are understood to make him eminently more suited to assuming positions of public leadership and responsibility than those of the female. Certainly the privileging of male over female attributes in the public domain has made it very difficult for women to be taken seriously as potential candidates for public office. It has also meant that a uniquely female contribution to public debate and decision-making has been conspicuously lacking.

Indeed, I would argue that the current, increasingly controversial process of neo-liberal economic globalisation, accompanied by growing levels of militarisation, reflects the present male domi-

---

[39] Heaphy, Donovan and Weeks (2002), "Sex, Money and the Kitchen Sink" in Stevi Jackson and Sue Scott (eds.), *Gender — A Sociological Reader*, Routledge.

nance of global political and economic decision-making structures. The core values of individualism and competition promoted within the neo-liberal economic model can legitimately be regarded as representing an essentially male value system. The emphasis within the sphere of international relations placed on building defence capacity through establishing military alliances and engaging in massive military expenditure, can also be seen as uniquely male preoccupations. I believe that women's under-representation within global power structures has meant that the core value of co-operation, so strongly associated with a female value system, is not sufficiently reflected in key international economic and political decision-making.

The sharp dichotomy I am drawing between male and female value systems may not be helpful as it appears to promote an "essentialist" view of both sexes, and to suggest, for example, that women have a monopoly on co-operative behaviour. I do not subscribe to a model of biological determinism, or to the notion that biological factors exclusively account for the differences in cognitive and behavioural styles between men and women. Social psychologists have suggested that processes of social and cultural conditioning play an important role in shaping the cognitive and behavioural patterns of males and females, and in influencing the ways in which they engage with the world around them. This means that although biological factors may predispose men and women to behave in particular ways, social and cultural influences can mediate these tendencies and can encourage certain modes of behaviour over others. Carol Gilligan's seminal research on gender and moral reasoning involved listening to girls and, to a lesser degree, boys, as they discussed moral problems.[40] Gilligan concluded that girls have a "different voice" when discussing moral issues, emphasising relationships and care, in contrast with boys' preoccupation with individual rights and abstract principles of justice. However, while Gilligan's earlier work appeared to suggest that there are actual empirical differences in modes of

---

[40] Carol Gilligan, *In a Different Voice*.

moral reasoning between the sexes, her more recent work appears to acknowledge that the same individual (male or female) may use both voices, mixing them as "contrapuntal" themes.[41]

If one accepts the finding that men and women can move between different modes of reasoning and behaving, the challenge for further research then is to identify the conditions and influences that encourage certain modes of thinking and behaving over others. Such an approach would accept the fundamental and essential differences between men and women. However, it would also work with the dualities that exist within individuals to ensure that the "masculine" and the "feminine" potentialities within each person were allowed full expression, rather than being constrained within restrictive sex-role stereotypes. For example, in *Making the Difference*, a path-breaking ethnography of class and gender relations among secondary school students in Australia, R.W. Connell et al.[42] argued that there are multiple masculinities, some hegemonic and others submerged or marginalised; it was claimed that the patterns are contradictory and continually negotiated. The authors also pointed to varied forms of femininity, ranging from the "emphasised" to less visible forms.

If we accept that the traditional paradigm of hegemonic masculinity has encouraged men to compete, to dominate and to control, then we need to begin to change popular consciousness so that the qualities of compassion, nurturing and co-operation become equally synonymous with male and female behaviour. As far as women are concerned, attempts at changing popular consciousness would need to encourage women to take more initiative, and to seek opportunities for leadership and for the positive exercise of authority. As a society we must begin to elaborate models of masculinity and femininity that allow for a more equitable distribution of power — personal, social, cultural and political — between men and women, in both the public and private

---

[41] Carol Gilligan et al. (eds.) (1989), *Making Connections: The Relational Worlds of Adolescent Girls at Emma Williard School*, Troy, NY: Emma Williard School.

[42] R.W. Connell et al (1982), *Making the Difference*, Boston: Allen & Unwin.

spheres. A quiet revolution is already occurring in the domestic sphere where fathers are increasingly assuming a more active role in the direct care of their children. This social trend needs to be strengthened and encouraged and will hopefully allow for a reverse trend to occur where women will be freed up to a greater extent to participate more actively in public life. The gains of one sex should not be at the expense of the other. Rather, men and women should be equally represented in the public and private spheres and the particular strengths of each sex should be brought to bear on the activities within each sphere.

In conclusion, I would argue that gender equality is, and must be, an essential feature of a just society. I cannot point to any society in the world where I believe true gender equality has yet been achieved, although important advances have been made. However, Ireland's record in this regard sadly lags well behind that of other EU member states. How can we change this? How can we begin to move towards becoming the kind of society where true equality exists, where the possibilities and opportunities available to an individual are not contingent on gender? It seems to me that cultural change, or changes in popular consciousness, must precede any substantive change in practice or policy-making in our society. The broad changes in popular consciousness are already underway but need a much greater impetus behind them, particularly in this country. A range of forces are mobilising behind the "equality agenda" to push for legislative and social changes in respect of disabled people, minority ethnic groups, gay people, immigrants and refugees and other excluded groups. Women must add their voices and their energies to this growing social movement and ensure that the issue of gender equality forms an important part of the equality agenda, as it cuts across so many other issues. This will require a significant revitalisation of the feminist movement in this country, and significant networking with other interest groups to identify common concerns. Finally, it is my hope that women will not find themselves fighting this battle alone, but that they will be joined by many enlightened men who see their own liberation as intimately bound up with the liberation of women.

20

RESPECTING PATIENTS

Dr Leonard Condren

The world of modern medicine is a very different place to the world I entered when I graduated in medicine from UCD in 1977. Today we have extraordinary technologies at our disposal. MRI (magnetic resonance imaging) scanners allow us to take virtual photographs of areas of the body that were previously inaccessible with conventional imaging techniques. Fiberoptic scopes allow us to directly visualise the interior of the body and have facilitated the development of the speciality of keyhole surgery. Today we treat peptic ulcers with antibiotics and drugs that reduce acid secretion in the stomach, whereas back in the 1970s many ulcer sufferers were treated by elective surgery.

There is so much that we can do today that was not even dreamed of in 1977. However, these technological advances carry hidden dangers. My chief concern is that medical technology has become so fascinating that we are in danger of becoming mesmerised by it. We are in danger of being overly preoccupied with computers, scanners and scopes to the detriment of our focus on the predicament of the sick person.

It is more important than ever before that we do not lose sight of the seminal event that underpins all of this technologically driven activity. That seminal event is the consultation, which is that very special occasion when a person visits the doctor to discuss their health concerns. The words of Sir James Spence, a distinguished paediatrician from Newcastle-upon-Tyne, are as relevant today as they were in 1949 when he discussed the role of the doctor and the central importance of the consultation in the following words:

> The real work of a doctor is . . . not an affair of health centres, or public clinics, or operating theatres, or laboratories, or hospital beds. These techniques have their place in medicine, but they are not medicine. The essential unit of medical practice is the occasion when, in the intimacy of the consulting room or sick room, a person who is ill, or believes himself to be ill, seeks the advice of a doctor whom he trusts. This is a consultation and all else in the practice of medicine derives from it.[43]

Medical consultations take place in various environments. They occur in hospital outpatient departments. They occur in curtained cubicles in accident and emergency departments. Sometimes they occur in hospital corridors. Consultations also occur in consultants' private rooms located in leafy Georgian squares or state-of-the-art modern private hospitals. However, most medical consultations that occur each day in Ireland take place in general practice. That is the medical environment that I know best.

The general practice consultation is usually an encounter between two people who already know each other. In some cases, they may have known each other for many years. GPs provide care that is very personal to individuals and families that sometimes encompasses most of the extended family. However, the general practice consultation is more than an unsophisticated chat between two people that are relatively at ease in each other's

---

[43] Spence, James, "The Need for Understanding the Individual as a Part of the Training and Functions of Doctors and Nurses", Speech delivered at a conference on mental health held in March 1949; Reprinted in *The Purpose and Practice of Medicine: Selections from the Writings of Sir James Spence*, London: Oxford University Press, 1960, pp. 273–4.

company. In order for the encounter to be effective, the two people must trust and respect each other.

Despite the various medical scandals of recent years, most people still trust their own GP. People can be very critical of the medical profession in general: "Doctors don't listen"; "They're too busy and don't have time to talk to you"; "They're only interested in making money". Yet amidst all this negative comment people usually say *"My doctor is different"*.

This trust has not been automatically given to GPs. It has been earned. GPs realised a long time ago that the values and attitudes that traditionally existed in the hospital setting were totally inappropriate in the community. First of all, the setting for the encounter is very different. GPs usually practice from conventional houses that have been converted into medical centres, which is a considerably less threatening environment than the hospital. GPs are very accessible to the people they serve. Also, the relationship between the person and their GP is a more adult relationship than the traditional model of medical paternalism. The dialogue between the person and their GP is more a dialogue of equals. The glue that holds the relationship together is the mutual trust engendered by their previous encounters with each other.

Let us look at a sample of this glue. I remember a house call I made twenty years ago. A frantic mother who was very worried about her daughter, an only child, requested the call. The mother was a widow and lived with her daughter in a local authority flat. The child was in her bed in her own bedroom surrounded by her teddy bears and cuddly toys. She was pale, sweaty and clearly in some distress. I had never seen her so ill before. Following a brief medical examination, it was clear to me that the child was suffering from meningitis and would have to be admitted to hospital without delay. I beckoned the mother outside to tell her the difficult news. I was afraid that, if I told her the news in front of her daughter, she might lose her already brittle composure and cause further alarm to the child. I then went back into the child and told her what we had to do. I gave her an injection of penicillin. She had a terror of needles but allowed me to administer the injection without too much protest. The ambulance came promptly and she was admitted to hospital. She survived the illness without residual complications.

Ever since that episode, the trust of that family in me became awesome. I knew they trusted me before this episode but now the trust was automatic and implicit in the way they received nearly everything I said. The mother often reminisced with me about the day I saved her daughter's life. Several years later, when the daughter grew into adulthood and left home, she continued to attend me in my surgery in Ballyfermot even though she lived on the far side of the city. She trusted me so much that she was prepared to traverse the city of Dublin to see me rather than attend a doctor nearer to home.

The essential point I am making is that people trust their GP and that the bond of trust strengthens over time. Just think of some of the things that people trust their doctors with. GPs hear extraordinary stories from people. We hear very private and intimate details about different events in people's lives. People allow us to do extraordinary things to them. They allow us to draw blood from them. Women trust us to perform very intimate examinations such as breast examinations and smear tests. None of this activity would be remotely possible if people did not trust their doctors.

People often say that their GP is a very nice doctor. It is always pleasant to receive a compliment but being nice to people is not really the point. Charlatans can also be very nice to people. The more fundamental value that should drive the relationship is respect. Respect is made manifest by old-fashioned virtues such as courtesy and good manners. Shaking a person's hand when you greet them and addressing them by name are all part of the trappings of respect.

But real respect is manifest at a more subtle level. The GP respects a person by engaging with them, empathising with them and actively listening to them. Active listening is a much more dynamic process than simply hearing what a person says. It means paying attention to the totality of what the person is communicating to you. It also means observing the person's body language as they speak.

Respect also implies that the doctor is not dismissive of people because they have a poor vocabulary or are lacking in formal education. Let me give you an example. A woman used to attend me on a very frequent basis. She came from a background of poverty and left school prematurely at twelve years of age. She married young and that marriage subsequently failed. She had difficulty managing her children, some of whom had become quite rowdy. My particular memory of her was that she often used phrases like; "I'm probably saying this all wrong" or "I don't have the words to say this proper".

Perhaps the fault was mine that she felt it necessary to say such things to me; however, she was one of the most intelligent people I knew. She may have lacked formal education and may not have been very socially skilled but I knew that when she spoke I did not have to ask any questions. I knew that if I simply sat and listened, she would unfold her story clearly before me. In contrast I have known many people over the years who were very socially skilled and were so-called well educated, yet would not have possessed this woman's intelligence or level of insight.

Respecting the person also means that you respect their autonomy. I can recall an encounter with a middle-aged woman that occurred several years ago. She was a widow who had an intense fear of hospitals. One day she attended me with pain in her chest that was clearly not cardiac in origin. However, I really was not sure what was causing her pain and suggested that I refer her for an x-ray. After a great deal of persuasion, she agreed and the x-ray report duly came back the following week. I discussed the x-ray findings with her. The x-ray revealed that a shadow was present in one of her lungs and further x-rays were recommended to establish the nature of the shadow. After further persuasion, she agreed to undergo the additional x-ray studies. These studies indicated that a mass was present in the lung but she would need to be referred to a respiratory physician for further evaluation. It was not possible to out-rule the possibility that the mass might be due to cancer. I discussed the findings and recommendations with her but she was adamant in her refusal to go to hospital.

Parallel to this exercise in autonomy was a simultaneous negotiation in giving or denying consent. At each point of decision along our journey together, she was the one with the ultimate power to decide if the next step would be taken. Respect for this woman meant respecting her autonomy rather than retreating into medical paternalism and saying that I knew what was best for her.

Respect for the person also means being non-judgemental about that person within the consultation. The doctor is entitled to his or her own views on matters outside of the consulting room, but these attitudes and views must be discreetly left outside the room when the consultation begins. If that stance is not adopted, how is the doctor supposed to engage with a person who indulges in activity that the doctor disapproves of?

For example, the doctor might well feel that a person presenting with a sexually transmitted disease has been irresponsible but it serves no useful purpose for such thoughts or feelings to be expressed. Such a person requires empathy and understanding because they may be experiencing strong feelings of self-loathing and guilt. Any negative comments from the doctor may intensify such negative feelings, especially if the person happens to be young.

One of the finest compliments I ever received was from a young woman with a very troubled past. Some of the trouble in her past was of her own creation and she had left a significant amount of wreckage behind her in terms of human relationships. One day she said to me; "I don't really know how you feel about any of the things I have told you about myself but I never felt that you sat in judgement on my actions. That's why I always felt that I could come back and see you again when I needed to."

Respecting people may also mean that the doctor has to deal with a person who they do not particularly like. It would require the tolerance and patience of a saint to be able to like everybody. Some people are not very likeable and some are downright disagreeable but such negative feelings within the doctor need to be held in check. It should be possible for a mature doctor to engage in a consultation with anybody even though he or she might not relish the prospect of bringing that person home for tea.

Sometimes the GP may be more severely challenged and will have to deal with individuals with an odious past. Wife beaters, violent, abusive alcoholics and sex offenders are all figures of hate in society but such hate has no place in the consulting room. The convicted paedophile is also worthy of respect within the confines of the medical consultation. He also has a right to receive medical care and any feelings the doctor might have about the paedophile's abhorrent deeds are irrelevant to the encounter. I would put it even more strongly and say that if such thoughts or feelings within the doctor were made explicit in the consultation, then the paedophile should terminate the consultation. Every person, irrespective of their past deeds, is deserving of respect within the consultation.

Respecting people also means that you tell them the truth. This becomes crucially important when talking to people who are terminally ill. In the past, many doctors evaded the truth and spoke in half-truths and white lies for the best possible motives. Their understanding was that they were acting in the person's best interests and wanted to save the person from the discomfort and distress of facing the awfulness of their predicament. We now know differently. The difficulty with telling white lies is that once the truth becomes known the person may feel that the bond of trust between them and their doctor has been damaged. This realisation can have significant negative effects for the dying person and can increase their sense of isolation and loneliness.

Respecting the dying person also means telling the truth with sensitivity. Some doctors say that they always tell the truth. But there are different ways of telling. Giving a person the unvarnished truth without empathising with their predicament can be just as insensitive as telling them nothing. It is also true that some people really do not want to hear bad news and are more content to live out their final days in denial. If opportunities have arisen for the person to be given the truth and the offer has not been taken it is appropriate not to disturb that state of denial. The overriding principle here is that the person's desire for information be respected and that whatever is said by the doctor must be the truth.

Since we have touched on the subject of denial it would be an act of denial on my part if this discussion on truth and respect did not mention the significance of the Harold Shipman case. Many doctors uttered private gasps when the details about Shipman began to emerge. The possibility dawned for many of us that the repercussions of Shipman's actions could extend beyond his victims and their families and open up a chasm of mistrust between people and their doctors.

The Shipman case has prompted calls for increased regulation and scrutiny of the medical profession, but would that really be in the best interests of the individual person's ongoing relationship with their doctor? It is also reasonable to question the motives of those who might push for such change. Some vested interests wish to curb the power of the medical profession and may see the Shipman case as the profession's Achilles heel.

Harold Shipman murdered people that trusted him implicitly and yet we know of no clear motivation for his crimes. My personal experience post-Shipman is that most people still trust their personal doctor and rightly regard this serial killer as a sinister deviant. To introduce new rules and regulations in response to the actions of such a person would be an inappropriate response and would be an additional tragedy.

I am now in the second half of my professional career and I suspect that I am likely to witness further technical triumphs in the field of medicine. The rate of progress in medical science seems to accelerate exponentially each year. No doubt some of these advances will generate their own difficulties. For example, when we acquired the technology to keep seriously ill people alive on life-support systems, questions arose about who should benefit from such treatment. That advance also created the dilemma of when to turn such equipment off and also the very fundamental question of who has the right to make such decisions. It is quite likely that the dilemmas of the future will be even more challenging.

I suspect that the medical landscape of the future will look very different to the present. I believe that the fundamental importance of the consultation needs to be re-asserted and that this special encounter should take its proper place centre-stage and not be shunted off to the wings by soulless technology. Perhaps our medical educators need to expand the horizons of the doctors of the future by emphasising the ethical dimension to conducting a medical consultation. The consultation is the seminal event in medical practice and I fear that it is insufficiently appreciated.

21

LAWFUL EUTHANASIA IN IRELAND? A PERSPECTIVE ON A UNIVERSAL MEDICO-ETHICAL DILEMMA

Dr Ubaldus de Vries

INTRODUCTION

Discussions on euthanasia often revolve around the question of whether a right to euthanasia should exist. Should a person have a right to determine not only when to stop living, but to require or permit another to assist him in executing his decision? The Supreme Court decision in *Re A Ward of Court* did not go as far as to assign a right to euthanasia.[44] Nevertheless, it allowed the patient to die with reference to the so-called "double effect" rationale: allowing having treatment stopped, she could pass away peacefully. Euthanasia — an intentional act to bring about the death of a person — was a step too far. In this Chapter, I seek to explain that euthanasia can be lawful as an *ultimum remedium*. I defend the position that euthanasia can find its place within the doctor–patient relationship. I consider this argument by reference to an analysis of the *Ward of Court* case and to certain general notions that are used in the debate about euthanasia, such as autonomy

---

[44] [1996] 2 I.R. 79; [1995] 2 I.L.R.M. 401.

and self-determination, the sanctity of life principle and the principle of beneficence.

THE *WARD OF COURT* CASE

The case is the result of a tragic accident that befell the ward of court in 1972. She had undergone minor gynaecological surgery under general anaesthetic but human error caused her to suffer severe brain damage. As a result, she lived her life in a near permanent vegetative state (near PVS). Completely dependent on others, she required full-time nursing care. She was artificially fed, first through a nasogastric tube, which was later replaced by a gastronomy tube because the former distressed her too much. The gastronomy tube had to be surgically inserted several times because the ward had the habit, either consciously or through pain reflexes, of pulling out the tube. Her cognitive functions were virtually extinct. The patient was made a ward of court in 1974. In 1995, the family of the ward applied to the High Court for an order to stop the hospital from artificially feeding their daughter so that she could die. Exercising his so-called *parens patriae* jurisdiction, Judge Lynch consented, on behalf of the ward, to the termination of the artificial nourishment. A majority of the Supreme Court confirmed the decision. The court's decision contains many important aspects. I focus on the court's deliberations on the patient's alleged right to die.

Wardship

Wardship means that the President of the High Court is assigned the duty of looking after a person's interests when that person is no longer capable of looking after his interests himself. Usually this would extend to managing the property of a person. The law demands that the court exercises its wardship jurisdiction, subject to the provisions of the Constitution. Thus, the court must have regard to the constitutional rights of the ward and interpret these rights in accordance with the Constitution. At least three constitutional rights may be referred to: (i) the right to self-determination,

(ii) the right to life, which the State is obliged to protect and vindicate, and (iii) the right to bodily integrity.[45]

Autonomy

The court's argumentation starts from the premise that although the patient is a ward of court, she has not lost her right to self-determination, which stems from her autonomy. The right to equality demands this.[46] However, since she is unable to exercise her right to self-determination, it is up to the President of the Court under his *parens patriae* jurisdiction to do this on her behalf. In doing so, he may have "due regard to differences of capacity, physical and moral, and of social function".[47]

The Right to Life

One implication of the right to self-determination which the court had to consider was whether the ward had the right to determine the ending of her own life. Would a right to self-determination go as far as to include a right to die? The court held that the right to life does not include a right to die by commission. The Chief Justice stated that the right to life merely implies the right to have nature take its course and to die a natural death. Alternatively, he held it to mean the right "not to have life artificially maintained by the provision of nourishment by abnormal artificial means, which have no curative effect and which is intended merely to prolong life".[48] Thus, the right to die is confined to the natural

---

[45] The right to life is referred to in art. 40.3.2° of the Constitution; the right to self-determination and bodily integrity are unenumerated rights. The courts have read these rights into the Constitution by reference to art. 40.3.1°.

[46] Art. 40.1 of the Constitution.

[47] Art. 40.1, second sentence.

[48] [1996] 2 I.R. 79 at 124.

process of dying and does not include the right to have life terminated or death accelerated.[49]

The Right to Bodily Integrity and Privacy

The alternative interpretation that the court offered of the right to self-determination is particularly relevant in the doctor–patient relationship. The right to self-determination implies a right to bodily integrity. The right to bodily integrity means that no person is to tolerate the involuntary violation of one's body. In medicine, this means that patients ought to consent to treatment proposed by the doctor. This consent must be an informed consent.[50]

In the context of the *Ward of Court* case, a preliminary issue arose, which was whether the artificial nourishment through a gastronomy tube could be regarded as medical treatment, for which consent ought to be given. The Supreme Court agreed that a gastronomy tube is surgically inserted into the stomach and that this may be regarded as intrusive and an interference with one's bodily integrity. This meant that nourishment is to be regarded as medical treatment and not merely as medical care.[51] The court also held that the condition the ward was in, was one where her life was artificially maintained by the type of medical treatment that had no curative effect — she would remain in that condition so long she was nourished.

Hamilton CJ held that, accordingly, the ward's right to bodily integrity would imply that were she to be *compos mentis* she has the right to decide to forego treatment. Hamilton CJ explained that it requires the State to recognise that competent adults are

---

[49] The House of Lords and the European Court of Human Rights held a similar position in the *Pretty* case. Both courts held that the right to life refers to the state being prohibited from depriving a subject of his life and having, furthermore, a positive duty to vindicate and protect that life. *Regina (Pretty) v. Director of Public Prosecutions, Secretary of State for the Home Department*, [2001] U.K.H.L. 61; *Pretty v. The UK*, Unreported, E.C.H.R. 29 April 2002.

[50] See also the analysis of Judge Denham in her judgment; [1996] 2 I.R. 79 at 156.

[51] Ibid. at 114 and 124–125.

free to make decisions relating to life and death. This would in fact mean, according to the Chief Justice, that "a competent adult if terminally ill has the right to forego or discontinue life-saving treatment".[52] Hamilton CJ considered the ward to be terminally ill, since without artificial nourishment she would die.

The Vindication of her Constitutional Rights

The particular nature of "wardship" means that the court acts and makes decision in name and on behalf of the ward. In doing so, the court must have regard to the constitutional rights of the ward and consider whether these rights conflict with the Constitution as a whole.

The analysis of the judgment so far indicates that the ward has a constitutional right to withdraw treatment. This stems from her right to life as well as her right to bodily integrity. These rights do not conflict: the right to bodily integrity does not mean she can request to be killed by commission; the right is a "shield" against interference and not a "sword" to demand interference. Thus the right to bodily integrity does not conflict with the right to life such as it was interpreted by the court: the right to have life take its course. Nor did the right to withdraw treatment conflict with other provisions of the Constitution.

It was then the task of the court to exercise this right on her behalf. But how could the court come to a decision? It is clear that the court was guided by medical opinion, in respect to both the mental state of the patient and how that had come about, the prospects of recovery and the worth of the care and treatment she was provided with. The court accepted the evidence that the ward was in near PVS, that there was no hope of recovery and that the care and treatment she was provided with had no curative effect.

The Chief Justice adopted the so-called best-interest test, balancing between the benefits (a prolonged life) and burdens (a

---

[52] The Chief Justice meant that a patient who is *compos mentis* is entitled to refuse treatment of an illness even if this would lead to his death. The illness does not necessarily need to be a terminal illness.

grievously restricted existence), approaching the matter from the standpoint of prudent and loving parent.[53] In doing so, the Chief Justice agreed with the President of the High Court that on the basis of the evidence and the ward's situation it would be in her best interest that treatment should be withdrawn. Judge O'Flaherty added to this that "the ward may be alive but she has no life at all".[54] With it, the learned judge meant that although the ward was in a near PVS, she would hardly have any feelings of pleasure or displeasure, nor would she realise or know the condition she was in. He approved the words of the trial judge, who stated that if the minimal cognitive function she may still possess "includes an inkling of her catastrophic position, then I am satisfied that that would be a terrible torment to her and her situation would be worse than if she were fully PVS".[55]

The court knew one dissenting opinion. Judge Egan held that since the ward had some cognitive function left, permission to withdraw treatment should not be given. He wondered whether withdrawal would still be permissible if a slightly more cognitive function would exist; where would the line be drawn? He thought it too dangerous to allow the termination of life in cases where patients had some cognitive function left.

The Kernel Lies in "Suffering"

The *Ward of Court* case shows that the treatment at life's end, and the accompanying notion of a right to die, are firmly rooted within the doctor–patient relationship. The reason that this is so is

---

[53] A minority of the Supreme Court adopted a so-called "substituted-judgment" test. Here, the court considers what the ward herself would have wanted were she to have one lucid moment. This demands, of course, some evidence from the past about the opinion of the ward on questions about life and death (expressed in, for example, a living will or advance directive). These were virtually absent in the case. For a detailed analysis of this aspect; see Tomkin and McAuley "Re A Ward of Court: Legal Analysis", op. cit., p. 45.

[54] [1996] 2 I.R. 79 at 130.

[55] Ibid.

the emphasis placed on the physical and mental state of the patient and his "suffering". The nature and extent of the suffering informs the doctor about the proportionality of his actions and the availability of any reasonable alternatives. These are both clinical considerations.

So far, the court has recognised what is really a matter of common medical practice. Conscientious doctors do and always have regarded the alleviation of suffering as one of their primary medical objectives. The usual paradigm though in which this operates is referred to as the doctrine of "double effect".

Instead of leaving this as it is, a general and humane point can be made, which is that at some stages of acute suffering life may be ended intentionally, if and when a patient requests this or his or her situation is akin to that of the ward of court. This does not mean the recognition of a right to euthanasia but rather to create exceptions to a general rule. Thus, euthanasia remains unlawful, unless there are exceptional circumstances. I believe that a justification for this position can be found in the medical context itself, with reference to the role of the doctor and the nature of the doctor–patient relationship. In doing so, I refer to the principle of autonomy, the sanctity of life principle and the principle of beneficence.

AUTONOMY AND THE DOCTOR–PATIENT RELATIONSHIP

The principle of autonomy and the attendant right to self-determination each refer to a person having the freedom to determine what he or she can do with life. Be clear though, in a debate about euthanasia, that autonomy does not refer to the freedom to end one's own life. Suicide is the act that gives expression to this freedom and is not legally prohibited in most countries, including Ireland. It rather refers to whether one person can legally assist another to die. Can autonomy be extended to others? The argument goes that criminalising the person who carries out euthanasia or assists in a suicide obstructs the autonomy of the person seeking death. This leads to the proposition that "the state must not do anything that obstructs the exercise of what is regarded as a fundamental freedom".[56] In euthanasia, the autonomy of one person, thus, depends on another person. The latter is, in one way, used as a tool, albeit a willing tool, to effect the decisions that flow from the exercise of autonomy of the former.

The Doctor–Patient Relationship

In any discussion on euthanasia and assisted suicide, the doctor is assumed to be the instrument by which death is achieved. Within the doctor–patient relationship, the patient's autonomy is regarded by some as existing in the patient defining his own needs and determine the nature of the satisfaction of those needs (a patronage system or patient-centred model).[57] Others prefer a so-called collegiate system or doctor-centred model. Here the doctor determines the needs of the patient and the manner in which they are satisfied.[58] The notions of consent and informed consent illustrate that there is a mixture between these two extremes. We have given recognition to the patient as a party to the relationship and regard him no longer as a mere object of the relationship. The moral notion of autonomy is expressed in the legal notion of (informed) consent. Thus, no person can be treated if that person does not consent to such treatment. The patient can only consent if he is also properly informed about the alternative treatment options and their effects. The rule on consent has given room to allow people to refuse treatment or have treatment withdrawn with the possible, or intended, consequence that death will follow. This has been one of the key aspects of the decision in *In Re a Ward of Court*.

---

[56] See Griffiths et. al. (1998), *Euthanasia and Law in the Netherlands,* Amsterdam University Press, p. 168.

[57] Cosmetic surgery for aesthetic reasons may be a case in point.

[58] See, for example, Turner (1987), *Medical Power and Social Knowledge*, London, p. 136–137; Johnson (1972), *Professions and Power*, London, p. 45–46. See also U. de Vries (1996), *Professional Negligence Reconsidered*, PhD Dissertation, Dublin City University, Ireland, p. 128 (unpublished).

Thus, autonomy in medicine gives shape and recognition to our right to bodily integrity: autonomy is a shield against unlawful invasion of our body; not a sword by which we can demand the invasion of our body. How would this apply to euthanasia?

Within the doctor–patient relationship, autonomy cannot be regarded as a patient having a right to expect a doctor to assist him with the materialisation of his death wish (it is not a sword). Rather, autonomy is to mean the freedom to consult with a doctor about the options of treatment at life's end and the ability to understand and consent to an option that may deliberately and intentionally end his life. From this, it follows that autonomy cannot be a basis to justify an overt right to euthanasia on demand.

BENEFICENCE

Autonomy as embedded within the doctor–patient relationship is closely connected to the principle of beneficence. In medicine, it refers to a duty to alleviate pain and ease suffering. The duty of beneficence has undergone change within the medico-ethical context. The duty that a doctor must treat a patient at all costs has lost weight; current medical ethics does not hold on to the preservation of life at all costs. Beneficence may now be regarded as a duty not to do harm, which can include a duty to stop treating (rather than starting to treat) or to choose for a course of action that actually ends the patient's life if this means that suffering can be relieved. Euthanasia and assisted suicide, it could be argued, is an act of beneficence in that it is done to avoid the harm of continuing suffering: the double effect rationale. This is not to say that the principle of beneficence must be seen as an independent justification for a right to euthanasia. It merely suggests that doctors in some cases can be morally justified in proposing a course of action on the basis of sound medico-ethical grounds.

THE SANCTITY OF LIFE

The changing notion of beneficence is, on its turn, closely related to the sanctity of life principle. The traditional sanctity of life principle refers to the prohibition of the intentional taking of life in any circumstance. The principle transcends an individual right of a person, or his autonomy, to request death or to commit suicide.[59] It also prevents forms of passive euthanasia. Thus, life is sacrosanct, and cannot be touched. Whether we live or die is not for us to judge upon — it is in the hands of fate or providence. That this can be accompanied with unbearable suffering, of all sorts, is a burden we must bear. However, as medicine improved and insight was gained into the treatment at life's end, which also included a different notion of death and dying, the sanctity of that life became subject to a different meaning.

In the context of treatment of life's end, the sanctity of life principle no longer refers only to life itself but also to its quality. We started to accept the idea that life need not be unnecessarily prolonged for the sake of life itself. The English decision in *Airedale N.H.S. Trust v. Bland* is illustrative.[60]

In the *Bland* case, the plaintiff had been one of the Liverpool soccer supporters who were caught up in a melee, which was the result of an overcrowded stand (the Hillsborough disaster). He suffered severe brain injury that led him to enter a permanent vegetative state. The question was whether the doctors were allowed to stop treating Anthony Bland while he was still alive but unconscious and incapable of giving his consent to the treatment and care he was given.

The House of Lords allowed the doctors to stop treating him. The test was whether continuing treatment would be in "the best interest" of the patient. Relying on medical opinion, the Law Lords accepted that Tony Bland was not aware of anything and that there was no prospect of improving his situation. This con-

---

[59] The previous prohibition on euthanasia and assisted suicide was based on the idea that the criminal element of euthanasia or assisted suicide was not aimed at the life of an individual but rather to life in general: the sanctity of life.

[60] [1993] A.C. 789; [1993] 2 W.L.R. 350. For an analysis of the case, see Keown "Courting Euthanasia? Tony Bland and the Law Lords", *Ethics & Medicine*, 9:3 (1993), p. 36.

vinced them that stopping treatment was legally and ethically justified. One Law Lord stated that "the continued treatment of Anthony Bland can no longer serve to maintain that combination of manifold characteristics which we call a personality".[61]

The case broke new grounds, since it abandoned the idea that life has an intrinsic value, irrespective of its quality. It also abandoned, in one way, the "double effect" doctrine, as the Law Lords knew that the withdrawal of treatment was intended to kill Anthony Bland, contrary to relieving his suffering, albeit by omission. The decision in the *Ward of Court* case also underscored this new interpretation of the sanctity of life principle. Judge Denham held that "a view that life must be preserved at all costs does not sanctify life".[62] She continued, stating that "to care for the dying, to love and cherish them, and to free them from the suffering rather than simply to postpone death, is to have fundamental respect for the sanctity of life and its end".[63]

At this point it is interesting to note that the Supreme Court in the *Ward of Court* case went a step further than the House of Lords in *Bland* when allowing the withdrawal of treatment on the basis of the "best interest" test. Whereas Anthony Bland had no cognitive function left whatsoever, the ward of court had been in a *near* permanent vegetative state; she had some cognitive function left, albeit negligible. Nevertheless, the court held that her quality of life was not an issue; she was alive but "she ha[d] no life at all".[64] The Irish Supreme Court thus entered into a grey area in which the quality of life argument (within the context of the sanctity of life) has become much more value-laden. It remains to be seen whether this will pose ethical problems in the future.

---

[61] [1993] 2 W.L.R. 350 at p. 400, *per* Lord Mustill.

[62] [1996] 1 I.R. 79 at 161.

[63] Ibid.

[64] [1995] 2 I.L.R.M. 401.Ibid., at p. 432 *per* O'Flaherty J.

CONCLUSION

At the outset of this article, I raised the fundamental question as to whether euthanasia should be lawful. I explained that it should remain an exception to a general rule. There should be no right to euthanasia. I defended this argument by reference to the principle of autonomy and its place within the doctor–patient relationship, as well as to the principle of beneficence and the sanctity of life.

Within the doctor–patient relationship, autonomy is to be understood as the right to consent to treatment such as proposed by a doctor. It does not mean that a patient has the right to ask from a doctor whatever he desires. The doctor must act, and does act, on the basis of what he believes is in the best interest of the patient. His medical skill and knowledge informs him of this. The patient may or may not consent to this. This also means that there are limits of what a doctor can do. Anything that falls outside the medical realm cannot provide for sufficient grounds to come to a determination that leads to euthanasia or assisted suicide.

Since the doctor has among his tasks the duty to relieve suffering, the principle of beneficence provides a moral rationale to choose a course of action, which leads to the death of a patient. This rationale is closely linked to the changing notion of the sanctity of life principle with the emphasis on the quality of life rather than life itself. Society cannot take, or should not take, the perhaps psychological barrier to assign its citizens a right to euthanasia. It is to be preferred not to allow for a right to euthanasia, unless certain circumstances present themselves. To accept otherwise, we effectively say that the State has a right to take life away from its citizens on grounds other than those which are currently accepted.

22

ETHICS AND THE MEDIA IN IRELAND

Frank Shouldice

When first discussing the theme of ethics in the media with editor John Scally, I wondered what working definition of ethics he had in mind. "Between right and wrong," he suggested, providing the widest frame of reference. It was a good starting point.

People may not trust journalists but they do trust the news. There is a widespread perception that news speaks for itself, that the mystical process of newsmaking is inherently neutral. News simply *happens*.

It is a dubious premise that does not stand up. Events don't go straight from thin air to screen or print and there are a lot of helping hands along the way. News production may be a collective effort but every journalist faces ethical choices within that process.

Facts are part of any story — preferably an integral part! — but issues of tone, treatment, motivation and timing each carry a decisive weight. And it is here that ethical questions usually arise, addressing whether journalistic practices are right, wrong or loitering the prairie somewhere between.

Theories of Ethics in Journalism have been explored at length elsewhere. In the broader scheme, ethical issues range from legislative restrictions (censorship, libel), to conglomeration and concentration of media (monopolies, conflicts of interest), to the cultural bias of news values, to the unidirectional flow of information, along with attendant commercial pressures of presenting news to an increasingly distracted audience.

All of these pressures chip away at the edifice of news as actuality. News values may be an abstract notion but editors and journalists have to make personal calls on every story. What is objectivity, one might argue, but a disputed fact?

For instance, when Seamus Brennan was first challenged over an unpaid departmental bill for £5,000 on whiskey and cigars from Aer Rianta, his initial response was not whether he was the minister involved but why the revelation was timed in such a way. Indeed as a deregulation-oriented Transport Minister, his ongoing conflict with Aer Rianta made for an interesting backdrop to the *Sunday Independent* exposé. Many felt his response was quite inadequate but who could deny that he had a point?

If the alleged non-payment took place ten years ago, why was it being reported in November 2002? If sources were aware of an alleged misuse of power, why was the story let sit for nine years? Assuming non-payment for goods is wrong, what is evident here is that reporting a wrongful act is not as straightforward as it seems.

More perniciously, consider the recent controversy surrounding coverage of a clerical child abuse case. Fr Ivan Payne, tried and convicted on paedophile charges was, on release from prison, tracked by *The Star* (a story later picked up by the *Irish Mirror*, *Evening Herald* and the *Joe Duffy Show* on RTE) in a campaign to highlight the risk of recidivism. Paedophilia is patently wrong but does that make *The Star* (and others) right? If there was any consistency here, should the same media feel obliged to monitor — and possibly pursue — every sex offender on release? Would it be right to do so? And if doing so would be ethically wrong, what made it right in this particular case?

The standard response of editors and broadcasters who take a strong stand on particular issues is that they are acting in the public interest. Ethically, this presumes accession to the moral high ground. Acting in the public interest is, however, a matter of interpretation. Do media interests ever adopt unpopular causes? Or would a commercial enterprise target "a public enemy" if it didn't pay to do so? None of this is as black and white as first appears.

Commentators speak of news "product" because like everything else for sale it must survive the marketplace. Making the product digestible does not necessarily require "Freddie Starr Ate My Hamster" every day but it is adequate for news products to render a palatable *version* of the world.

Sticking by the holy trinity of journalism — to inform, educate and entertain — you cannot have one without the other. So, if we are going to get the world warts-and-all, we can expect a higher-than-average application of beauty spots. Plenty of sugar to make the medicine go down. The ethical doublespeak here is that the adjusted picture — *do not adjust your set, we'll do it for you* — is unvarnished truth, representing the world as it really is.

Rooted here is one of the media's unstated functions: to reassure the public. For every newsmaking explosion, murder, rape and horrific — but photogenic — catastrophe, we need to be reassured that our world is not a completely hopeless case. So after we receive grim warnings of a huge asteroid hurtling our way or scientific links between margarine and cancer, we develop — or have little choice acquiring — incommensurate interest in David Beckham's next haircut, Ronan Keating becoming James Dean, the successful mating of chimps/rhinos at Dublin zoo or Pierce Brosnan/Samantha Mumba/Chris de Burgh expressing pride in their "Irishness" (although the media may leave Chris de Burgh aside from national feelgood duties for some time yet).

To some extent, this balancing act merely reflects a human limit to depressing events. Let the sun shine brighter on TV or fill the picture pages with beautiful people. The home truth — neatly ignored — is that we are more interested in *virtual* reality. You want realism? Watch the soaps.

A QUESTION OF VALUES

News values are always open to debate but evidence suggests that economics is increasingly dominant at the expense of other influences. Reality does bite. *The Irish Times* newspaper, run as a not-for-profit trust, had its commercial meltdown in 2002. The long-term impact is yet to be assessed but the presence of Robbie Williams across four columns on Page Three is an ominous sign.

We constantly hear about the "dumbing down" of news — even sparking a mini-revolt by weather staff at RTE — but the principle argument is that market forces dictate. The obvious effect is to trivialise, simplify — or ignore — serious, complex events. The dividing lines between information and education are being colonised by a market-driven demand for entertainment.

So if actuality is the earthquake that happened in remote Armenia, news is the televised earthquake that happened in scenic San Francisco. Both earthquakes did occur but while we recall spectacular re-runs of a car crashing on a distended section of the Oakland Bay Bridge, might anyone tell us what or where exactly Armenia is?

The cultural bias of coverage does not seem like an issue of right or wrong but it does raise ethical issues. Can we be so concerned by what happens to some people and remain oblivious when the very same misfortune happens to others?

Ethics and Best Practice

Despite a constantly changing environment, the fourth estate remains relevant and strong. It adapts marvellously. Media evolve into different forms — many newspapers now run subscription-based websites — but news production is still imbued with a sense of crusade. Sky News trumpets the way — just press the red button on your keypad to *play a part* in the news — with a steadily dumber ITN chasing close behind.

Ethical questions usually relate to how journalists perform their role. Politicians — and others facing the heat — are quick to accuse "the media" of a witch hunt but seasoned campaigners are skilled manipulators themselves. Opportunism works both ways and when the media are a means to an end, ethics will not get in the way.

Journalism itself is often portrayed as a sort of public watch-dog. The implicit assumption is that it is a school built on its own code of good practice. Significantly, the PR agencies employed by public bodies and companies are all peopled by former journalists who know how to play the game. Surely such an easy switch from gamekeeper to poacher questions the very ethics of what journalism stands for. Should its ethics stand alone, like a set of unwritten laws? Or does possessing media savvy simply translate into playing the system for the highest bidder?

Irish politicians have developed such a *nous* for TV news cameras that RTE, TV3 and TG4 tend to swallow "photo ops" hook, line and sinker. During the last election campaign, Bertie Ahern's whirlwind tour of the country was designed to *look* dynamic without *being* dynamic. He would arrive at one end of town, walk at speed through the main streets in a torpor of flesh-pressing and hop back in the campaign bus at the other end. The fact that he said nothing and did nothing on these visits was glossed over. News crews ran after him and Fianna Fáil got the coverage they wanted.

Is it a matter of right or wrong that journalists on the campaign trail allowed themselves to get suckered into this type of promotion? Despite pleadings of politicians under fire, the manipulative use of the media broadens the ethical debate into who actually controls production. The point is that the stooges are sometimes *behind* the camera.

Consider live TV coverage of the Dáil, deemed so unexcitingly mundane that labelling it "national service broadcasting" is the only justification for giving it air time. Shots are limited to pre-ordained angles but effectively, each image is constructed to enhance reality. If a deputy falls asleep during a parliamentary debate, the TV crew is not allowed film him/her in isolation. Elected representatives usually manipulate proceedings in a way to suggest the chamber is fuller than it actually is. Deputies "doughnut" around party colleagues so that on TV it looks like everybody is present. A truer shot would reveal deputies frequently addressing nobody. Who does the current practice serve? And is it ethical?

It occurred to me that even with seventeen years' experience working in journalism, there are many who deal more directly with ethical theory in practice. For every editor of a national or provincial newspaper, routine decisions raise ethical issues head-on — what stories to run, what stories to drop, what angle to take, what headline, what to lead with on Page One, with what photo. These are just some of the innumerable decisions that make up daily production in any newsroom.

John Scally explained that he was open to hearing editors relate their position. When it came to the crunch, however, no editor was keen to take a busman's holiday and write 3,000 words on the ethics of journalism. To find leading editors too busy is hardly a revelation. What does surprise however is that nobody *seized* such a rare opportunity to air the issue, if even to present the editorial side.

There is a detachment here which, not unlike many aspects of modern life, practically excludes reflection on the way things are. If you do the job, why ask why? Just get on with it. Working under twin pressures of time and space, the central assumption is that media practices prove themselves. They are the way they are because the market decides. That, in every way, is the bottom line.

FREELANCING

My own experience in journalism is largely as a freelancer. Apart from staffing with an Irish newspaper in New York for several years, most of my print work has been in feature writing, social issues, sport and the arts. I've also directed for television and scripted for radio.

Freelancing is not everyone's cup of tea. This is not a cross to bear — journalists are a breed prone to complaint — but like any competitive arena where ego is involved, it can be a bruising business. Maybe this is just part of the whittling-down process. Those who can handle rejection are the ones to survive; everyone else can discover the inner child or shuffle into PR.

Through the years, I have been fortunate to deal with fine editors across print and broadcast media who, even under pressure, have been able to manage, encourage and reject in an even-handed way. That is quite a skill. And there are others who treat you as replaceable as you are and calmly remind you that it is a buyer's market.

The analogy between freelancers and actors is useful enough. Actors get knocked back all the time and the option is to stay with it or quit. For most freelancers the assorted knockbacks — non-decision on submissions, rejected stories, commissioned stories subsequently dropped, payment (very late, reduced or sometimes not at all), phone calls/e-mails unreturned, messages ignored, ideas pinched — are accepted as coming with the territory.

Of course, the volume and pressure of production means a newsroom cannot iron out every wrinkle that comes its way. Save for a number of exceptions, however, editors are not particularly interested in getting involved in the mountain of small problems accumulating outside their door. They often find themselves wedged between management and staff, steering work practices they themselves would find unacceptable.

It is not unusual for freelancers to spend more time trying to get paid for a particular job than the time spent actually working on it. Much of this is avoidable and you would think there must be a better way for the business to look after its practitioners.

Typically, the magazine, newspaper or radio station you worked for may have misplaced yet another re-submitted invoice. Just when you begin to wonder if you really want to put yourself through this, you read/hear the same publication/programme cry hoarsely about someone somewhere getting a raw deal.

That said, the pitfalls of freelancing are not an exclusively Irish experience. Working in Sydney fourteen years ago, I went for a job interview with a magazine that was setting up in the suburban deadzone of Parramatta. Another interviewee sat in the room be-side me, linked by handcuffs to a police officer. The handcuffed girl and I were going for the same job, so if mere availability was an advantage, I fancied my chances.

I was interviewed by the magazine's managing editor, a bearded gent full of enthusiasm. He made a dismissive joke about the girl, adding that she wasn't getting out of jail for three years. He commissioned me for work but over a period of months, despite numerous phone calls and lost invoices, I never got paid. The cheques were always "coming". When it got beyond a joke, I took the ghost train to Parramatta to find that the magazine had disappeared. All gone.

One to put down to experience, I guessed. Several months later, I saw a familiar bearded face on television. I had to laugh when I realised the entrepreneur had made the news on *Australia's Most Wanted* as a big-time con-man. I accepted with wry relief that I was one of his lesser quarries.

Actually, I'm not sure to what occupational category — if any — journalism rightly belongs. For some reason it is usually described as a profession but investing it with a status usually applied to academic faculties — law, medicine, engineering — is dubious self-promotion. Why should journalists aspire to such an exclusive grouping?

THE MEDIA IN A CHANGING LANDSCAPE

There is no question that societal changes in Ireland have altered the media's role. Traditionally, people sought direction from the Catholic Church but the Church has lost its platform. So who provides direction now? Elected representatives appear unfit for the role, while both other "estates" – the army/police and the judiciary — are too removed from the people. National heroes — always a temporary mantle — can frequently inspire but seldom lead.

Indeed, the marginalisation of traditional leaders opens new ground for opinion-makers. Within a vacuum, the baton, as such, has passed to the media. Print columnists and editorial writers have become the secular pulpiteers of the modern era, setting the agenda, stating set positions. If you want guidance on any aspect of life — child-rearing, politics, sex, drink, drugs, buying a house — you will find it here, usually offered as information, education or entertainment but more often driven by a particular viewpoint.

This is an ego business and writing a regular column would appeal to many journalists. For a couple of years, I wrote one myself — the "Journeyman" column in *Ireland on Sunday*. However, the ethical issue here goes far wider than personal ramblings.

Changes to the social order have enhanced the media's potential to influence public opinion. Journalists do not have to seek re-election or take policy decisions. We/they do not represent an institution. We/they have a freedom to judge those in authority but exercising that freedom is a power with minimal responsibility. The hurler on the ditch seldom has to stand *for* anything.

In sports journalism, for example, it is possible to excoriate a football manager over poor results or bad performances — take Mick McCarthy's recent departure from the Irish team. A journalist is free to take pot shots without ever having to make an actual decision or carry responsibility for a mistake. Arguably, this is offset by high wages for the manager (which compensates him for the pressures of bad press) but the same dynamic applies where no money is involved. From that safe vantage, it is a forum wide open to abuse.

Yet somewhere in the hallowed stereotype, the inveterate journo — not unlike the gumshoe — is portrayed as a flawed hero with right on his/her side. More Eddie Shoestring than Terminator. In an ethical dreamworld, journalism always protects the innocent and exposes the guilty. The real world is a bit more complicated. Besides, the holy trinity of newsmaking leaves only so much space for chasing baddies — libel laws alone are very restrictive although it is hard to say who libel actually protects in Ireland.

On the rare occasions when editors prompt readers to march on the home of a named abuser/criminal, they might do well to remember that in most democracies the fourth estate is not an arm of the judiciary. There is something wrong about being *so* right, calling all the shots to double up as judge and jury.

In political journalism, evidence of corruption, hypocrisy or ineptitude is not always enough. Public representatives are cushioned by libel laws and whenever rural politicians get bad press — such as Michael Lowry, Joe Jacob, Denis Foley — a typical reaction is to galvanise local support against a (Dublin) media conspiracy. Others in the line of fire prefer to send a party hitter onto

"Questions without Answers" and reduce political debate to pub chat without the drink.

Maybe Ireland is still too small and we don't have the appetite to go digging too deep. Irish journalism produces relatively little investigative reporting. The public is already mystified or bored with Ansbacher, a multi-million euro tax swindle involving many of the country's elite. Newspapers and broadcasters contend they do not have the resources for long-term investigative work — and if the tribunals are anything to go by, digging deep is indeed a slow and expensive train.

We have a poor record here. When Irish journalist Susan O'Keeffe researched irregularities within the Irish meat industry for *World in Action*, her findings led to the damning but ineffectual Beef Tribunal. Everything she researched was verified. As a result, she was not celebrated as an ethical reporter doing a fine job but was instead threatened with imprisonment for failing to reveal her sources.

The state prosecution against her was unsuccessful but the fact that it happened at all punches holes in what Irish media can aspire to be. In this case, the reporter who courageously did justice to the bold cliché of journalism was the only one to risk jail from the Beef Tribunal. It is something to turn the ethics of Irish journalism on its head.

If we are serious about upholding ethics in journalism, what is to protect the next investigative reporter who finds something she/he is not supposed to? And if shooting the messenger is fundamentally wrong, why was the general public so indifferent to Susan O'Keeffe's plight?

Journalism in Ireland does not belong in the same gallery as Parramatta's finest, but the business here, certainly from a freelance point of view, could take a close look at itself from inside-out. The potential for journalism to do good remains strong but external pressures put the bottom line ahead of most considerations. Those who are intimately involved with ethical decisions daily may not wish to discuss it but as Susan O'Keeffe and many others have discovered, even things that ain't broke often need fixing.

23

ETHICS IN SPORT

Dermot Earley

The first thought that comes to mind on the subject of ethics in sport is that it involves a sense of fairness in all sporting activities. It also reminds us that sporting contests, in whatever code or discipline, are undertaken by complying with the rules of the game, match or event, and that fitness, skill, teamwork, tactics and motivation are the ingredients by which the contest is played out to a decision. Ethics also demands respect for the game being played, as well as for opponents, and that integrity, justice and democracy prevail in the playing, administration and adjudicating of all sports. Finally, there is a responsibility on all participants, including spectators, to uphold the characteristics and spirit — the ethos — of each particular sport.

In defining sport, two words stand out: fun and contest. Sport is about enjoyment, satisfaction, fulfilment and requires some skill and a certain amount of physical exercise. Where there is a contest, then a trial of skill and perhaps greater physical endeavour are required. When sport is a pastime, a leisure activity, then the ethics of sport — the conduct of the participants — is courteous, correct, by the rules and without the pressure of having to win. When sport is professional or organised professionally and winning ensures further success, then ethical issues are tested more often.

"The hand of God and the head of Diego" is one of the most famous incidents of ethical dimensions in world sport. This was the explanation given by Diego Maradona of Argentina after he deflected the ball with his hand over the advancing England goalkeeper Peter Shilton in the World Cup semi-finals. His goal helped Argentina to victory over England and they went on to take the World Cup in that competition. Should that goal have been allowed? Did the officials see hand contact? Did Maradona handle the ball deliberately? Should he have owned up immediately?

In the Munster Senior Gaelic Football Championship game between Tipperary and Kerry some years back, a Kerry forward shot for goal from close range. His effort crashed into the side netting but to the astonishment of the Tipperary players the umpire raised the green flag and a goal was awarded. In this instance, it appeared that the players from both teams knew that the ball had gone wide but the match referee, going on the action and advice of the umpire, allowed "the goal" to stand. Should a Kerry player have indicated to the referee that the ball was wide?

The most talked about recent "ethical" incident occurred in the final moments of the European Rugby Cup Final of 2002. Munster were trailing Leicester and were driving hard for their opponents' line when they were awarded a set scrum some five metres out from goal. It was crucial to win this ball and set up a final drive for possible victory. As the Munster scrum-half was about to put the ball into the scrum, his opposing wing forward, with a deliberate hand action, knocked the ball from his grasp into the Leicester scrum and the ball was lost to Munster. The referee had taken up a position opposite the incoming ball and did not see the incident. Scrum half Peter Stringer and the Munster players who saw what happened were incensed. Neil Back of Leicester who knocked the ball from Stringer's grasp won a European championship medal some moments later. Was Back's action ethical?

Ethics is the study of human actions in respect of what is right or wrong. The actions of individuals or groups and teams supply the subject matter of ethics. There must be a distinction between actions that are voluntary — that are intentional — and actions that are involuntary. Ethics deals with those voluntary, intentional actions. Spur-of-the-moment deliberate action is different from reflex action as reflex action does not involve new calculation. Most controversies and debates are generated by the perceived unethical spur-of-the-moment deliberate action and by the unwillingness of a participant to play by the rules of the game.

Sport provides an opportunity for young and old to express themselves, generally in public, to learn new skills, to become more confident, to deal with adversity, to support and depend on team mates, to show leadership, to follow leaders, to delight in winning and to acknowledge the unsuccessful. Sport teaches us about life. The late Chief Justice Liam Hamilton, patron of the International Club of the Football Association of Ireland commented at the launch of the Code of Ethics for Under Age Soccer in Ireland that

> Ethical behaviour is the litmus test of a civilised society, the principles of fair play, care for others and simply being a good sport are the building blocks of successful teams, communities and ultimately of a peaceful nation. As well as being fun sport is a good training ground for life.

This training ground for life can work in strange ways. As a youngster, at national school in West Roscommon, and being taught by my father, I learned a solitary lesson in honesty through sport. One night we got particularly difficult sums which involved a combination of addition, subtraction, division and multiplication. If you made a mistake in the first part, then all subsequent calculations were wrong. Having your father as your teacher was often beneficial in that assistance at homework helped in clarification and in ensuring that correct procedures were followed. On this night, no help was sought or offered and the sums were completed. The next day as the method and answers were demonstrated on the blackboard, my dad asked all who got their sums right to put up their hands. My hand shot up. The teacher walked through the desks and looked at my copy and asked "is that the answer on the board". I said "no".

Nothing more was said until later than evening when, homework done, I got my boots to join the lads who were gathering outside to play football when my father said, "Where are you going?" I replied, "Out to play football." "No you are not," he said. "You told me a lie today. No football for you this evening." He didn't say another word. I stood at the kitchen window and watched my pals gather for the game and later could hear the shouts of encouragement and joy and groans of endeavour as my friends played their hearts out. It was the longest evening of my life and taught me a lesson. Never tell a lie. I have told this story often to young players encouraging honesty in all situations, including effort, and being fair in word and deed.

My father used sport in many ways to teach a lesson. One day during a geography class he picked up the football which was always inside the door of the classroom (the first one out the door took the ball at play time). By this simple action, the eyes of every boy were riveted upon him. For the next twenty minutes or so, he taught us everything about latitude and longitude. The ball was the earth and lines were drawn with chalk across and down the ball. In the end, we were all experts on plotting positions around the world and in the weeks that followed, as the games were played, great fun was had in kicking India or Africa or facing Australia towards the goal for a free kick. To this day, I can see my late father, ball balanced on the fingers of his left hand above his head, explaining the finer points of latitude and longitude.

From the rural classroom to the seat of government, sport can and has played a significant role. This can be very positive in the running of great world events like the World Cup and the Olympic Games. But sport can be a destructive force too, as anyone who has seen the bigotry of a Celtic/Rangers clash at first hand will testify.

Sport for me, though, has always been a unifying force and it can bring people together, create bridges, maintain contact with the outside world and be a release where tension and strife are the general daily diet. Another example of this mix of politics and sport was the boycott of South Africa by international sporting bodies during the apartheid regime. This was an action with which I did not agree, as I support the idea of influence through contact to change bad to good. Today India and Pakistan do not agree on many issues and are engaged in a war of attrition in Jammu and Kashmir but they still play cricket against one another and shake hands at the end of the game.

Sport can defuse tension and as a common interest create a bond that removes barriers. In 1975 on the Golan Heights between Syria and Israel, sport helped solve a potentially tricky situation. As part of the ceasefire agreement between both countries, an agreed number of soldiers, tanks and missile systems were allowed in the theatre to opposing forces. To ensure this was adhered to, the United Nations Military Observers inspected and counted these troops and systems every two weeks. Some of my colleagues went to a particular base where the commander would not co-operate and allow an inspection of his resources. This was in breach of the agreement but after much negotiation the observers got access to the commander's tent.

Once inside the tent, my colleagues noticed that there were pictures on the notice board of many English and European soccer players. Among them were Ray Clemence, Bobby Moore, Bobby Charlton, Johann Cruyff, Denis Law and others. A discussion on football took place and a ball was produced from behind a desk. The Syrian leader said he enjoyed playing football as a goalkeeper and all went outside to show their skills. The goals were two stones placed the correct distance apart and a challenge was thrown down to take a penalty. At this point, most of the soldiers in the camp had gathered at the sight of a possible contest. One of the Irish officers was chosen as the penalty taker and the Syrian commander took his place in goal.

As the ball was placed, a UN officer from the Soviet Union whispered in the ear of the penalty taker, "It might be prudent to miss." The kicker now had a problem. If he were to score, the commander's reputation would be tarnished in the eyes of his own troops. If he were to miss deliberately, it could be seen as an insult. So with great skill, he drove the ball hard and straight at the keeper, who parried the shot and gathered safely. The "supporters" were delighted and with handshakes all around there was no problem at all in carrying out that and all future inspections at that specific camp.

George Orwell in *The Sporting Spirit* wrote that "serious sport has nothing to do with fair play. It is bound up with hatred, jealousy, boastfulness, disregard for all rules and sadistic pleasure in witnessing violence; in other words it is war minus the shooting." Yes, sport can at times get "bound up" with some of the characteristics listed by Orwell but what is different from war (apart from the guns of course) is that there are rules by which the game is played and there is a policing system in place in most sports where the whistle of the official can end the action temporarily and allow for reappraisal, adjustment and the cooling of tempers. But what sport and war share are tactics and perhaps gamesmanship.

Tactics is about playing to your strength and having a series of plans to exploit the weaknesses of your opponents. Gamesmanship, as British writer Stephen Potter (1900–69) described in the title of a book, is *The Art of Winning Games without Actually Cheating*. Tactics are fully acceptable in any sport as long as rules are not broken but gamesmanship can be seen as exploiting or stretching the rules to the full extent. It is here that opportunities are taken by players to get that advantage by feigning injury, for example, in order to get time to recover from a hard bout of play. This type of activity is difficult to police and the responsibility rests with all participants in sport in such situations to have the right attitude to playing the game.

I.J. Cowan in *Conflict and Morality* (1995) quotes a story from *A Passage to India* by J.B.S. Haldane. He draws a contrast between the Old Testament story of Abraham and Isaac and a story from Hindu mythology of entry into heaven. After fighting battles and climbing the Himalayas, the survivors eventually were allowed into heaven but not before their leader had stood his ground and refused to abandon his dog. The lesson here is that one must not carry out actions that one regards as wrong even if commanded to do so by the gods.

Forty years ago, I played a juvenile game in the west of Ireland that was a close, hard-fought contest. My immediate opponent was a top class-player and I still remember the contest as we tried to better one another. Towards the end of the game, I broke clear and headed for goal. My opponent gave chase and put me under pressure. As I got closer to the posts, a coach from the opposing team roared continuously, "Pull him down, pull him down." Under pressure, I got my shot away and scored. As I jogged back outfield with my opponent close by, the coach roared, "Why didn't you pull him down?" My opponent stopped running and in a pleading voice and arms outstretched, he calmly said, "That's not how you play football."

Ethics in sport today throws up much more than just playing the game. Much is written and spoken about performance-enhancing substances, about the code of ethics and good practice for children's sport and about the behaviour of coaches, adults and parents in the promotion of sport for all. Thankfully through the sports councils and the organising bodies of all sports, there is a growing awareness of ethics in sport.

Sports of some nature are played in almost all countries of the world. Sport can be a great unifying force and an indication of the make-up of a people. Sport can express the character of a nation and national success gives an identity to its people by lifting that country onto the world stage. Sport has always had a very special place in the lives of most Irish people and our international success has helped to enhance our identity.

The European Sports Charter and Code of Ethics (Council of Europe, 1993) defines fair play as

> much more than playing within the rules. It incorporates the concepts of friendship, respect for others and always playing within the right spirit. Fair play is defined as a way of thinking, not just a way of behaving. It incorporates issues concerned with the elimination of cheating, gamesmanship, doping, violence (both physical and verbal), exploitation, unequal opportunities, excessive commercialisation and corruption.

In my lifetime in sport, there have been many disappointments, some successes, a few victories, but most of all it has been fun and enjoyable. Sport accommodates everyone: the player, the supporter, the organiser, the teacher, the coach and many more. For everyone, the greatest satisfaction is knowing that in victory or defeat you did your very best and were fair in all your actions.

24

WHEN WINNING IS NOT EVERYTHING: THE ETHICS OF SPORT

John Scally

Listen to a small child imitating his father's and mother's words, trying to get the sound right, the pitch and intonation, the vowels initially, and eventually after many a difficult battle those elusive consonants. Deep grammar or not — and the esteemed Mr Chomsky may well be correct about the structural mystery of language — what you are listening to is a young child trying to forge a link with generations past, present and future. Perhaps if there is one reason why so many adults with big brains remain fascinated with sport, it is because we all start off as little creatures playing those games and, like salmon heading back from the sea, we never lose a sense of where the stream starts: in memories strung together which continue to mesmerise us.

Sport, unique in its evocative hold on identity, take us back to that moment of initial fascination with the world when as small, imitative children we first swung a hurley or kicked a ball. I believe that the mystery of human selfhood is bound up with the mystery of sport: "How are we conscious?" and "How does sport affect us?" are probably parts of the same bigger question for many of us, but we cannot answer the first unless we answer the second. Roddy Doyle famously remarked that it was only while watching Ireland play in the World Cup in Italy in 1990 that he first realised he loved his country.

Jean-Paul Sartre wrote, "When man understands himself as free and wishes to use his freedom, then his activity is play." Sports and games have been an integral part of the human race for as long as there have been human beings. Through sport, people discover their strengths and find their limits. In games they discover their relationships to other people and shape their community. Sports and games have a special significance for the humanising of human beings.

No sociologist can ignore the power of Gaelic games in rural Ireland to harness the communal values of loyalty, self-discipline and sacrifice and all for the glory of the parish. They epitomise the importance of respect for place, memorably captured in Anthony Daly, the captain of the Clare hurling team, and his victory speech in 1997 when the Banner County emerged from decades in the wilderness to claim the Munster title: "We are no longer the Whipping Boys of Munster!"

MORE THAN A GAME?

As a boy growing up in Roscommon, Gaelic football was the battery that drove my imaginative life and dared me to see Roscommon in a very different light. Football provided an escape from people's problems and anxieties. It allowed us to dream of better days to come. Success, albeit at a very modest level, increased our self-esteem. We walked that little bit taller, talked just a little more boldly, and wore our blue and gold caps with pride. When the county team was doing well, it didn't seem to hurt as much if the price of cattle was abysmal or if the summer was wet and it was virtually impossible to save the hay or the turf.

Professor Liam Ryan has pointed out that the GAA has played a greater part in healing the many rifts which have threatened to rupture families and communities throughout history in the last century than the Catholic Church. Neighbours, for example, who had shot at one another in the Civil War displayed a greater de-

sire to forgive and forget when gathered around the goalposts
than when gathered around the altar. Yet apart from its immense
sociological significance, sport is important because, like music, it
gives a lot of pleasure to a lot of people.

FEVER PITCH

For the romantics among us, sport is a parable of life at its innocent best, the world as it ought to be, the ideal for a moment realised. Sport is an expression of optimism: enshrouding sports lov-
ers with a redemptive feeling, melting away depression, pain and
bitter disappointment, hinting at a bygone age of innocence and
values that no longer obtain. In this perspective, the Olympic
ideal, where the essential thing is not to have conquered but to
have fought well, has enduring significance.

As winds raged at 35 knots and played havoc with sailing
boats during the sailing competition at Punsan during the Seoul
Olympics in 1988, two sailors of the Singapore team, Joseph Chan
and Shaw Her, were thrown overboard when their boat capsized.
Lawrence Lemieux of Canada was sailing alone in the silver medal
position in a separate event when he saw the sailors in distress.
The Canadian rushed to Chan, who was exhausted from struggling against the strong currents in his heavy sailing jacket. By the
time Lemieux had completed his rescue attempt, he had lagged
way behind in his race. However, the Olympic ideal was revived
when the judges awarded Lemieux second place. Moreover, the
International Olympic committee presented him with a special
award for his gallantry. Asked about his heroism, Lemieux simply
said: "It's the first rule of sailing to help people in distress."

Nowhere was this Olympic ideal better captured than at the
Winter Olympics in Innsbruck in 1964. Italy's Eugenio Monti and
Sergio Siorapes were hot favourites to win gold in the two-man
bobsleigh event. But as they awaited their second run, the rank
outsiders of Tony Nash and Robin Nixon of the British team were
feeling at the bottom of the world. Following a sensational first

run, their sleigh had broken an axle bolt and it seemed inevitable that they would have to withdraw from the competition.

Monti had completed his second run and seeing the predicament of his opponents immediately stripped the bolt from his own sleigh and offered it to Nash. In one of the most dramatic upsets in the history of the competition, the British went on to win the gold while the Italian pair only got the bronze.

Throughout its history, the Davis Cup Competition has produced many colourful characters. No one typifies the true spirit of the Davis Cup better than the German Baron Gottfried von Cramm. In the 1937 semi-final in which America fought a titanic battle against the Germans, von Cramm faced Don Budge, with the matches tied at 2–2, to decide the result. In the prevailing Nazi fervour, the German was told to win it for "The Fatherland". The sets went 2–2 and in the deciding fifth, von Cramm took a 4–1 game lead. Budge pulled back to draw 4–4. The German took the lead again until the American levelled at 6–6. The German saved five match points as dusk fell before the American eventually won. Despite his disappointment, von Cramm was smiling when he came to the net and warmly congratulated his opponent on his magnificent play. The Americans went on to win the cup and a few months later, the Nazis arrested von Cramm on trumped-up charges. He was locked in jail for seven months before being drafted into the German army.

Sadly, such lofty ideals increasingly seem anachronistic given the spate of recent scandals which have blighted the image of sport. Who can forget the disgrace of the Tour de France in 1998? The saga of the Michelle de Bruin case also caused heartbreak and trauma for many who missed out on their beauty sleep to watch her medal-winning performances in Atlanta. Former Irish rugby star Neil Francis predicted that it was only a matter of time before an Irish rugby player died from the effects of drug abuse. Equally alarming were allegations that the practice of taking performance-enhancing substances is widespread in schools rugby in Ireland.

Yet why are we so surprised by these revelations? Back in 1988, the biggest talking point in the athletics world at the Seoul

Olympics came off the track with the disqualification of Canada's Ben Johnson after clocking 9.79 seconds in the 100-metre final when he tested positive for drugs.

A WINDOW INTO THE SOUL OF SOCIETY

Sport is a microcosm of society. If our language is part of who we are, our sports actually tell us who we are. When we know the way winners and losers are treated in sport and the way rules are enforced, then we know a great deal about the larger society in which it exists. Conversely, if we know the social, economic and political values of a society, we could make an inspired guess about how its sport is organised. The defects we find in sport — cheating, violence and drug abuse — are an integral part of the wider society.

Increasingly sport is becoming identified with the culture of the survival of the fittest. This involves subordinating everything else in sport to winning. This approach was encapsulated in the popular saying attributed to the famous American coach, Vince Lombardi, "Winning isn't all-important, it's the only thing."

Sports stars today are confronted by an environment which is complex, competitive and demanding. Their inherited values and ethics do not equip them to deal with the problem of drug abuse in sport. These issues confront our society in general but our ethical tradition offers us no ready answers. The result is moral uncertainty and confusion.

THE NEW CHEATING

Sport is too important to let it become a monster out of control. Do we really want a situation where gold medals in the Olympics are determined not by an athlete's natural ability but by the skills of their chemist?

The time for practical action has long since passed. We could hardly leave a better legacy to our children than consigning the use of drugs in sport to the dustbin of history. In January 2000, the Irish Sports Council took an important first step in this process with the introduction of its anti-doping programme. However, the debate must go wider than the issue of drugs.

In recent years, Irish society has had many nasty reminders of the ghosts of our past, like the unbearable horrors of child abuse in institutions run by Church and State. Sport does give similar power to a number of people like managers and mentors. Generally this power is exercised very responsibly and indeed a huge number of people heroically volunteer their time to help others develop their potential. However, as in other walks of life power brings the potential for abuse. Tragically, Irish swimming has learned this lesson the hard way.

In response, the then Minister for Sport and Youth Affairs Bernard Allen issued his Code of Ethics and Good Practice for Children's Sport in Ireland in 1996. Codes of ethics serve a number of valuable functions insofar as they help to order life, identify wrongdoers, educate and elucidate good practice. The assessment and evaluation preceding the formulation of a code are conducive to reflection and to fostering an awareness of the importance of responsible behaviour. Drawing up a code is an educational experience *per se*. Enforcing this code is much more difficult.

A code of ethics identifies those principles which govern its adherents and it declares a point of view from which their practice might be judged. A code makes explicit the ethical principles implicit in practice. However, it cannot hope to offer a permanent solution to the problems, because the issues change. Codes of ethics are a signpost, rather than *the* blueprint for good practice. Mr Allen's code did have good things to say — but they must be seen as the first words on the topic rather than the last.

In 1999, the then Minister for the Environment, Noel Dempsey, convened a major conference on a crucial issue of national concern — genetically modified foods — where all interested parties were given a platform to air their views. Perhaps the current Minister for Sport, John O'Donoghue, might as a first step convene such a conference on ethical issues in sport in Ireland. Sports people of the past and present, coaches, administrators, parents and other interested parties ought to have a forum to pool their insights. The focus ought not to be on apportioning blame for the sins of the past but on ensuring that abuse, chemical and otherwise, in sport becomes a bad, but distant, memory. This sickness screams out for both prevention and cure now.

THE DEMON DRINK

In recent years, there has also been controversy in Ireland about the GAA's policy of accepting sponsorship from alcohol companies. The former president of the GAA, Dr Mick Loftus has been a persistent critic of this position. Dr Loftus announced that he would not attend an All-Ireland hurling final again until the Guinness sponsorship of the hurling championship ended. Rugby too has been heavily sponsored by drink companies.

Sponsorship always raises potential ethical questions. Is it appropriate, for example, that crime programmes are sponsored by insurance companies who may have a vested interest in hyping people's fears about crime? Similarly, there are specific ethical issues involved in sponsorship raised by alcohol companies. Alcohol abuse is one of the biggest social problems in the country. No drug has caused more damage to Irish families than alcohol. There is an ever-growing mountain of statistical evidence to show that alcohol consumption is widespread among teenagers and even pre-teens. Of course, the Guinness sponsorship of the hurling championship does not force young people to drink alcohol. Yet it would be naïve in the extreme to think that executives of alcohol companies would fork out huge sums of money on sports sponsorship unless they were convinced that it would lead to a significant increase in their sales.

The GAA face other contentious issues. Sport has always been inextricably linked with the wider culture and has always had massive cultural implications in Ireland. At its best sport can bring people together. Think back to the way Catholics and Protestants united to support Barry McGuigan in the 1980s. Yet sport can also be an agent of division. In 1998, while Bertie Ahern and Tony Blair were negotiating the historic Good Friday agreement, the GAA continued its ban on members of the RUC or the British security forces playing Gaelic games.

From Me to We

According to Emile Zola, the purpose of democracy is to make people feel less different from each other. Sport should aspire to the same goal. If it is not, we must make it so. A noteworthy incident happened in Wimbledon 2002 when Aisam-Ul-Haq Quereshi, a Pakistani Muslim, and Amir Hadad, an Israeli Jew, teamed up to play in the doubles to promote peace between their two religions.

The romance of sport is its unpredictability: sport is possibly the only arena where David can still defeat Goliath. Sport can teach society an invaluable lesson — there is no need to overpower when you can outsmart.

But there is another meaning in sport. At its core, sport is a profoundly spiritual activity. It requires the individuals involved to surrender their self-interest for the greater good so that the whole adds up to more than the sum of its parts. Contemporary society places great emphasis on the rights of the individual. However, a proliferation of institutions from the European Union to the World Council of Churches bear testimony to the interdependence of humankind and stress co-operation and group action.

Sometimes people say that sport is a metaphor for life but sport is an *expression* of life, a single, sometimes glittering thread, which reflects the whole. Like life, though, sport is messy and unpredictable. Many companies spend small fortunes to be told that teamwork is a social engineering problem: take group a, add motivational technique b and achieve result c. This is a waste of time and money. Sport teaches us that the key to building a team, like that of building a community, is to blend individual talent with a heightened group consciousness.

The eighteenth-century theologian, Joseph Butler, pointed to the twin drives within all of us to self-love and benevolence, and claimed that ethics is not necessarily a matter of antagonism or inner struggle between these drives, but more a matter of achieving and maintaining the right balance between being ego-centred and ego-transcending. This offers a wonderful conceptual framework for a discussion on moral dilemmas; but how is this balance to be achieved in practice?

Moral obligation should be considered as a socially constructed practice, as something we learn through the actual experience of trying to live with other people. We are not social because we are moral: we are moral because we live together with others and therefore need periodically to account for who we are.

A number of approaches to duty are possible, one of the most famous of which is Immanuel Kant's idea of the "categorical imperative": "Act only according to that maxim by which you can at the same time will that it should become a universal law." Kant argued that each rational being has a worth and a dignity apart from any end to which she or he might serve as a means. In the Kantian scheme, rational beings invariably treat other rational beings the way they would like to be treated themselves, since to do otherwise involves inconsistency and to be inconsistent is anathema to rational beings. When we interact with other rational beings we are compelled to consider their worth as individuals. By treating them as a means (however good), we use them only for some purpose, thus shattering their right to be treated as an end.

Moral responsibility centres on providing an account of the rightness and wrongness of our conduct in the service of the self and service to the other. The basis of this account is found in our ability to reason together in a careful, precise, and rational fashion about the person's moral obligation or duties or character. The former concerns what one ought or ought not to do when confronted with a particular situation. The latter concerns what sort of person one ought to become, so that one not only acts rightly but is also a good, morally praiseworthy person.

Our society is rich in social practices such as medicine, education and sport and none of these tolerate radical individualism; one must work or play according to rules and sometimes in a team. Sport is crucial for young people — not just in terms of their physical and social development but for what it teaches them about meaning. Sport teaches us the power of oneness instead of the power of the one. It teaches us that we need to expand our minds and embrace a vision in which the group imperative takes precedence over individual glory: to move from thinking about "me" to thinking about "we" — because the most crucial lesson sport teaches us is that selflessness is the soul of teamwork. There is no me in team.

It is indeed right and fitting to conclude with a little parable. What matters in this life is more than winning for ourselves; what also matters is helping others to win, even if it means slowing down and changing our course.

Some years ago, at the Seattle Special Olympics, nine disabled contestants assembled at the starting line for the 100-yard dash. At the gun, they all took off in haste. Things were going according to plan until one little boy stumbled on the asphalt, fell, and started to cry. The other eight heard the boy cry. They slowed down and looked back. They all turned around and went back, every one of them. One girl with Down's syndrome bent down and kissed him and said, "This will make it better." Then all nine linked arms and walked together to the finish line. Everyone in the stadium stood and cheered.